LORD
FORGIVE ME...

BULLSHIT

BUT I WAS A ~~BUSINESS~~

CONSULTANT

This book is dedicated to all the psychopaths, drama queens and bullshitters, who knowingly or unknowingly, helped me write this story

LORD FORGIVE ME...

BUT I WAS A ~~BUSINESS~~ BULLSHIT CONSULTANT

ANTHONY BUNKO

Everything in this book is based on true events. Events which have
finally escaped kicking and screaming out of the twisted mind of an
individual who's been bent completely out of shape from sleeping
in cheap hotel rooms, strip-searched too many times in airports and
brainwashed into writing utter crap on unruly flip charts.

First impression: 2014

© Copyright Anthony Bunko and Y Lolfa Cyf., 2014

Cover design: Mark Phillips

ISBN: 978 184771 875 4

Published and printed in Wales
on paper from well-maintained forests by
Y Lolfa Cyf., Talybont, Ceredigion SY24 5HE
website www.ylolfa.com
e-mail ylolfa@ylolfa.com
tel 01970 832 304
fax 832 782

'Consultants are people who come down from the hill to shoot the wounded after the battle is over'

Someone much cleverer than me wrote that around tea-time in 1628. However, with my consultant's hat on, I am now going to change it a bit and claim it for myself... so... here goes...

'Consultants are individuals who drive down the mountain (usually in top of the range BMWs) to shoot fuck out of the injured after the battle is finished'

Fleeced off some dead bloke
and adapted by Anthony Bunko, May 2014

Now who's the clever one!

Contents

If I was still a consultant, I would have entitled this first chapter something exotic like, 'Setting the Scene', or 'Mobilization'. Why? Because that's what consultants name things to make them sound all brainy so they can charge lots of money. However, since I'm not a consultant any more I can call it what I like... and I do like crusty cheese and onion rolls so here goes:

1

Crusty Cheese
and Onion Rolls

I CAN PICTURE the scene. It's fifty years in the future. I have suddenly just passed away. But not to fret; I did go peacefully in my sleep after having three hours of experimental Viagra-free lovin' with one of my nineteen-year-old girlfriends, and her twin sister.

Still smiling like a Cheshire cat, I'm stood outside the Pearly Gates. Other recently deceased people also wait to be checked in. When I get to the front, Archangel Gabriel looks me up and down. He glances over a CV of my life.

'Not bad... not bad at all.' He nods his head several times. 'And... I see you are from Merthyr Tydfil in south Wales.' He scrunches his face up as if he's just sucked on a lemon. 'That's one, rough, old, tough old town.'

I nod.

'And you were a punk rocker back in '77.' He steps in closer and whispers, 'Jesus wanted to be one but his old man wouldn't let him. Instead he made him wear extra baggy flares and listen to Deep Purple.' He whistles the opening bars to 'Smoke on the Water' and reads on. 'And I see you're a writer, something of a literary genius (his words not mine!) You wrote the life story of Stuart Cable from the Stereophonics, *Demons and Cocktails*. Great read. He's in here, you know. He started his own band with Marc Bolan and Phil Lynott. The Hair Bear Bunch they are called... Bloody racket!'

My chest instinctively puffs out with a sense of pride. The old couple behind me, who apparently had been killed in a motorcar accident in the Swiss Alps, appear to be suitably impressed.

The Archangel thumbs quickly through the next few pages of my life. 'Bunko... this looks fine... just... fine-eeeeeee.' He glares at the last page. His nostrils expand; his left eyebrow touches the top of his forehead. 'Hang on just a minute. It says here that between 2000 and 2012... you were a... a...' his voice rises up several decibels, '... a business consultant.'

The old couple next to me move away as if they've seen a suspicious-looking man, with a long beard, dressed in a robe walking onto a plane holding a bomb with the fuse lit.

'Is this true?' Gabriel looks into my eyes. 'Did you really cross over to the dark side?'

I glance down at the floor and nod back. I can feel my cheeks glowing red.

Tutting loudly, he clicks his wings together. Two huge angel bouncers in monkey suits and flashing dickie-bows appear by my side. 'Take him away boys,' Gabriel announces. 'Throw him down below... with the rest of the evil lot... the politicians, the rock stars... airport security guards... metalwork teachers, most of the other people from Merthyr... and... that Mickey bloody Rourke.'

Before I could argue, they grab me under my arms and begin to drag me away.

'No... there's a mistake,' I yell. 'I belong here... I didn't want to be a consultant... they forced me... they made me... honest.'

'Stop!' Gabriel holds up his hand. The angel bouncers grind to a halt. He approaches me suspiciously. 'Is that true? Were you really forced to be a consultant? Made to go into small to medium-size businesses and talk in the tongues of buzzwords and draw unreadable pictures on flip charts whilst using copious amounts of Post-it notes... were you? Were you really forced against your will?'

Everything goes quiet. I feel everyone's eyes stare at me. They all wait. Wait with bated breath for my reply.

Should I 'exaggerate the truth'? Just keep a straight face and say yes. A technique I had been taught when training to be a consultant. I knew my reply would mean the difference between a life of comfort in heaven and an eternity of misery in hell.

Oh, fuck it. To be honest I'd had enough. Enough of all the lying. Enough of all the backstabbing, the cheating and trying to please lunatics. It was time to come clean.

'No,' I sigh. 'I wasn't forced... I wanted to be one.'

A suicide victim faints. Head-over-tit, she falls through a gap in the clouds. An angel dives down to rescue her from dying again.

'Take him away,' Gabriel screams, 'get him out of my sight.'

In an instant they push me down a long metal chute. I slide down and down into the darkness. With a bump, I land on the charcoal ground. Red hot flames dance all around me.

'Anthony Bunko, I presume?' Lucifer holds out his bony hand with black painted fingernails. He helps me up on to my feet. 'We've been expecting you.'

2

Enter the Dragon, Exit the Bog

THEY SAY YOU always remember exactly where you were and what you were doing when you first hear the news about some big, tragic world event. Like the day JFK got assassinated.

OK, sorry, that's a bad example. I was only a few months old at the time. So, I guess when the bullet entered the President's head I was probably eating, sleeping or pebble-dashing my nappies. But from what I've been told by my parents, the news received a similar reaction to that of the episode in the Seventies when JR from *Dallas* got knocked off! A worldwide outcry as people clambered to find out if Sue Ellen had fired the deadly shot from the library or was it Bobby Ewing with his big shirt collars and Colt 45 from the grassy knoll?

Conclusively, there are many other incidents I can actually hark back to. The morning Lady Diana died; I wandered around the Spar shop in my hometown of Merthyr Tydfil all blurry-eyed after a night out on the tiles. An old woman, clutching a bottle of Toilet Duck and a Cadbury's Creme Egg, stood in the aisle, crying her eyes out. 'It's terrible isn't it?' she wailed.

I was just about to say, 'Yeah, it's the worst fucking hangover I've ever had,' when I noticed the headline about the princess's death splashed all over the front page of the Welsh newspaper.

Fast forward to the biggest incident in my lifetime so far, September 11th 2001. I was running my first ever workshop. I will explain later in the book how bizarrely the events of that fateful day unfolded and why I've never looked at the actors Peter Cushing and Christopher Lee in the same light again.

However, it's not only bad stuff that gets locked away in our memory banks. Life-changing moments are stuck in there as well. And finally getting to the point, I had my very own life-changing moment, one, wet, Tuesday morning on March 14th 1999.

Let's start at the beginning. No, not from the time my grandfather got arrested for cattle rustling or from the day I was actually born. Let's go back to just before my eureka moment.

I'd had a crap day at work at the car part manufacturing factory in Ebbw Vale and it was still only 7.20 in the morning. In truth, it started hours earlier when my eight-year-old daughter, suffering from the mother of all chest colds, thought spewing green gunk up over her dad every fifteen minutes or so, would make her feel better. (Later in life I discovered, to my cost, giving her handfuls of money made her feel even better than that.)

Being her sick-magnet did the trick because she fell asleep in my arms. Me, smelling like a lump of gone-off cheese, managed to doze off for all of forty-five seconds before the alarm clock screamed at me to get up.

Driving through the dark and the rain to the factory didn't brighten my mood. I'd only just stepped in through the main door to find a million people (I do not exaggerate) waiting outside my office to share (give) their problems with (to) me.

First off, we had let our biggest customer down yet again. They weren't happy.

'Pissed right off,' my dispatch manager informed me as he strolled out of my office.

On top of that, our one-and-only paint plant had broken down.

'Completely fucked,' the maintenance guy grinned before he also departed from my office, leaving that 'monkey' firmly on my back. Of course, his team were all too busy making pretty graphs to fix the bloody thing.

Also, we had run out of one of our main components, for the assembly lines. And the icing on the cake, my best team leader, Jules, had been locked up in Ebbw Vale nick after she'd found out her husband was having an affair with the woman next door. Allegedly, she'd gone around the woman's house with a baseball bat and beaten her up.

I kid you not!

The frustrating part was, that really wasn't a particularly bad start to the day. Just a typical morning in the life of a thirty-seven-year-old production manager working in a steering column factory on top of a mountain in the bleakest part of south Wales in the middle of an extremely cold winter.

What really pisses me off is seeing those 'D' list celebrities on shows like 'I'm a Has-Been Get Me Outta Here!' Those morons think surviving in the 'handmade' jungle is tough. Well I'm telling you now, eating live grubs or having hairy spiders put in your mouth or getting put in a coffin with a pack of hungry rats is fuck-all to what I had to put up with on a daily basis. I would love to see Christopher Biggins trying to run a production meeting on a Monday morning. Or Carol bloody Thatcher trying to persuade the union reps they are actually supposed to do some fucking work and not just sit about in their union office drinking tea and eating HobNobs while moaning about everything.

So all in all, it had been a crappy week, a shitty month and an excrement of a year! The constant pressure took its toll. I looked a lot older than I did eighteen months before I started working there. I found myself stuck firmly in a thankless job, in a thankless industry, surrounded by thankless, ruthless people. No one took any responsibility for anything. Everyone blamed each other. Individuals excelled at ducking and diving and finger-pointing. They sent emails cc-ing everyman and his dog. In their minds, by sending an email to everyman and his dog meant they had washed their hands of any issues and it was now every other man and his dog's problem to sort out. And that every man and his dog, normally, meant me! These 'pass the buck' emailers often got promoted. This allowed them to duck and dive more but this time with even more authority and their own parking space.

Anyway, enough rambling, let's get back to my life-changing experience.

That morning, I managed to get through the first wave of morning chaos. I'd successfully calmed everyone down. I promised our customer I would ship their product out that morning at our cost. The paint plant was working again but not fully. The supplier's parts had arrived. However I couldn't do anything to help Jules, the team leader, unless I baked her a cake and hid a file, a false moustache and a fake passport in the middle of it.

Around 8.45 a.m. I decided to take ten minutes out of my day and hide in my very own special place. A place I could just sit and block out all the madness. Trap 3 in the staff toilets.

With trousers down, I sat contemplating why the hell I had taken this path in my life. At school I'd received reasonably good grades. Hang on, before I give out the wrong impression, I wasn't up there with the swots at the top end of the class. On the other hand, I wasn't playing with a bucket and spade in the clay class either. I sat squarely in the middle.

My unshakeable memory of my comprehensive education was as follows and in no particular order:

Nuns, bullying, rain, cod and chips, satchels, fighting, dissecting a frog, oxbow lakes, Miss Roberts (the sports teacher) and her camel toe, youth club, more rain, angry nuns, swings, cheap cider, bunking and a music teacher who hated music.

Everything else that went on there thankfully got deleted from my memory bank for ever.

Sport had been my thing. I played rugby, football and ran cross-country for the school. Then again, music became my real passion from my third year onwards, when Joe Strummer exploded into my life. Overnight, I transformed from a long-haired, greasy yob in flares to a short-haired, greasy punk in drainpipe trousers and a dead man's shirt I bought from Oxfam. My parents hated it.

To me punk was more than the music and the fashion. It was the 'I can fuckin' do that' attitude. It stayed with me ever since and is probably the reason I'm writing this book. It helped my creative side to suddenly pop out of its box.

I remember my careers officer asking me what I wanted to do on leaving school. He was a religious nutcase who wore a long, grey overcoat, even in the summer. No one ever saw his feet. He just floated about the school corridors, clutching a Bible and looking pervy.

'How do you fancy a life in the priesthood?' he asked. Apparently, he asked every other boy in the school the same thing. I'm not sure what he asked the girls. Maybe if they fancied a life in the nun-hood, or nun-scarf, or whatever it was called.

'No, sir... Adverts, sir,' I said. He looked disappointed with my reply. 'I like adverts... I would like to make them up for a living, sir.' Famous adverts of that time like the 'Smash them all to bits' fired my imagination.

The careers officer looked at me as if I had two heads and only one baseball cap. He shook his big, balding swede. 'Anthony, you would have to go to university to do something like that. And I don't think you are the university type. So if I was you, I would look at either going to work down the pit or in a local factory, or become a priest... all three are jobs for life.' He smirked insincerely.

Too young and inexperienced to argue and too shy to answer him back, I shrugged my shoulders. Looking back now I wish I'd yelled, 'Oh! What the fuck do you know? You don't know me. You've only talked to me for two minutes in five years, so how can you give me advice on what I should and shouldn't do for the rest of my life?' But it would have been pointless. I may as well have been talking to the cupboard. (That didn't have feet either.)

My mother and father, who I love to death, were never the type of parents to encourage me or my younger brother to look over the garden wall at a brand-new world. Everyone in our cold, damp lives worked in factories or down the pit. I wanted more.

But my future had already been mapped out even before I was born. There would be no sitting around in a room for me being creative in a think-tank team coming up with catchy slogans like 'A Mars a Day' or 'Shake and Vac'. Where I lived people didn't do stuff like that. No! There were only nine-to-five jobs, council houses, fish shops, bingo, workingmen's clubs, watching football on weekends, and the odd trip to Barry Island with the Legion Club in the summer. A lifetime of clocking in at seven, leaving the creative side of their brains at the gatehouse in a shoebox and picking it back up when it was home time.

That was our life in a working-class nutshell.

Yet, whatever my useless careers officer said, there was no way I was going to work down the pit. No disrespect to the millions of hard-working and wonderful miners who did it religiously every day of their working lives. Grown men going miles underground in little cages to dig for small lumps of coal to me wasn't natural. Down in the darkness with no toilets, where spiders the size of street fighters' fists and rats as big as cats roamed about freely. That wasn't for me. No way, no how! No thanks!

In the end, I got an apprenticeship in the Hoover washing machine factory in my hometown. My father was a big union rep in the company and I think he pulled some strings.

To be honest, I had a brilliant laugh there and made lifelong friends. There were five thousand people working there when I started. OK, 'working' was a bit of a misleading word. Thousands of people turned up every day and did as little as possible. A giant holiday camp with angry foremen roaming about instead of Redcoats, and curry days on Thursdays.

For my sins, I got slotted into the engineering category during my apprenticeship. I think mainly because I was crap at making and fixing things. On saying that, I was useless at any of the engineering stuff as well. I didn't really want to know about the workings of a combustion engine, and I didn't care two fucks how much damage was done to a twin-tub washing machine if dropped from six feet!

At least I got to wear a white coat and I didn't have to dig for coal and get covered in blue scars. But overall it did give me a trade. It gave me a grounding and structure and discipline in my life. And unquestionably, it gave me money.

After a few years pretending to understand washing machines, I blagged my way into a different company making office furniture. A family-owned business run by a throwback to the old iron masters. The finger and thumb company they called it, due to the fact so many people lost their digits operating the machinery.

I escaped with all my fingers and thumbs intact, but not all of my sanity. I tried a few other roles until that morning I sat in the bog, away from the enemy like a schoolboy hiding from the bullies.

Suddenly, from my china throne, I heard my name over the Tannoy system in the factory. I ignored it. It got repeated several times. 'Fuck!' Then I remembered. I was supposed to be on some kind of training workshop all day.

I rushed out of the toilets. I really didn't have time to spend all day in a room full of idiots who couldn't organise a piss-up in a brewery. I knew exactly what the problems were in our business. Our main supplier was crap. All of their deliveries were late, and when something did actually arrive, the quality was shoddier than a 1970s dubbed Chinese *Kung Fu* movie. To make matters worse, our logistics department let our suppliers get away with murder as long as they got a nice bottle of vino and a frozen turkey at Christmas.

On the plus side, our managing director Bruce McFuckin' Nutcase was always worth the entry fee alone. The most unpredictable bloke I've ever known. Completely fuckin' Mcbonkers with a sharp sarcastic tongue that could cut a twenty-stone man in half with a few choice words. He didn't suffer fools. Let me rephrase that. He didn't suffer anyone.

Months earlier, a guy from the Welsh Office turned up to

discuss exporting our products to Eastern Europe. He sat in the boardroom, dressed in a cheap suit, a Mickey Mouse tie and matching socks. Bruce sauntered in fifteen minutes late, slurping coffee and puffing on a huge cigar (even though it was a non-smoking factory). He took one look at the guy and grunted, 'I'm not spending all day listening to that cunt...' He marched out leaving the guy stunned and me trying unsuccessfully to keep a straight face.

Bruce's twenty-two-year-old model of a secretary gave me a 'you are fucked' stare then carried on painting her fingernails. I slipped quietly into the boardroom. All the directors of doom were there. Debra, the human resource creature with full-on moustache and sideburns, sat talking bollocks with Kevin, the slimy, logistic twat. Shaun, the maintenance director, whose motto, 'Don't fuck with it, just leave it to break down and then we'll blame somebody else', sat in the corner trying to look intelligent while struggling to do the crossword in the *Daily Star*.

'Fuckin' hiding again, Bunko,' Bruce snarled at me.

Bright red, I poured myself a glass of water. Then the 'life-changing incident' happened. All my JFKs, JRs, September 11ths and poor Lady Diana lying crushed in the Paris underground, arrived simultaneously like number nine buses. In he walked. No, not walked, glided. Like a demi-god in a short-sleeved blue shirt, immaculately pressed cream chinos, and brown polished shoes. In his hand, he held a tan briefcase with a small dragon emblazed in one corner.

'Hi, I'm Silver Fox...' (of course, that wasn't his real name but in this book it is) ... 'I'm a business consultant.' He shook everyone's hand. 'Let's start.'

He placed the case on the table and opened it up. I half-expected a gold glow to light up his face like John Travolta in *Pulp Fiction*. He pulled out some pens, and a pack of Post-it notes. They weren't your everyday, run of the mill, Post-it notes. Not the usual, yellow, rectangular type. No way! These were every colour of the rainbow Post-it notes, and different shapes as well. Stars, hearts. Some which looked like Mister Blobby.

He meant business.

Without hesitation, he headed straight into a presentation full of colourful slides. He included interesting 'war' stories about his experiences of working in industries like ours. I knew exactly what he was talking about. However, looking at the faces of the other thick twats in the room, I could tell they were away with the fairies. They didn't have a clue.

After a coffee break, we came back to find he had laid out an exercise using Stickle Bricks. Everyone quickly glanced across at Bruce. We all waited for him to tell the consultant to stick the bricks where the sun didn't shine. But not only did Bruce get involved, he actually spent most of the game laughing and joking. Well, except when he went mental and called Len, the financial controller, a 'stupid fat cunt' and actually threatened to sack him for getting something wrong in the game.

The Silver Fox amazed me. He pulled buzzwords out of the air like a magician pulling white, goofy rabbits out of a top hat. He bandied words about like 'seven wastes', 'non-value added time' and 'customer satisfaction'. He made us draw pictures of what our futures would look and feel like.

My future didn't look bright or orange. It looked more like shit-coloured, and smelt even worse. I wanted to add a sketch of the *Titanic* sinking.

He then put us working in pairs, working in fours, and then back working in one big group. He reminded me of a sheepdog controlling the flock. He answered direct questions with another question. He stretched our thinking. Most importantly he kept Bruce interested.

After the last coffee break, we came back, to find him standing by the flip chart. A serious look took over his face.

'OK,' he said, turning the paper over. 'Here is what I believe is wrong with the business.' He pointed to the flip chart. 'All the directors are wankers and Anthony is great.' No, he didn't say that, but that's what he should have bloody said.

Instead, there was a long list of issues. He emphasised the following points as the first thing to sort out. 'Your main suppliers are not good enough and Logistics need to be more aggressive.'

I wanted to jump up and shout, 'I told them all that ages ago, but no one would listen to me. No one ever does.'

'You dull prick,' Bruce pointed at Slimy Kevin, the director in charge of Logistics. 'I knew it was your fault.'

'No... no,' The Silver Fox piped up. 'It's not the person, it's the process which is at fault.'

Again, everyone stared at Bruce. He went quiet for a few seconds. Then he did something I never thought I would see. He started clapping. 'You're right... it's not that stupid prick's fault... it's all the stupid pricks' fault.' Maybe a Freudian slip of the tongue, maybe not. 'But we will sort it out,' he growled, 'won't we?'

Everyone nodded.

The consultant came up with a simple action plan of how we were going to improve things and move forward. As normal my name got pencilled in to fix most of the points.

He thanked everyone for the session. I helped him carry his bags back down to his car. It wasn't the flash vehicle I expected, but a three-year-old Ford Mondeo. Our directors all had top of the range models like BMWs or Land Rovers. Bruce had a different car for every day of the week, which he drove in on every day of the week, just because he could.

'What are you doing for the rest of the week?' I asked.

'I'm working from home tomorrow.' The Silver Fox started putting his items into the boot, 'then we have a team-building day on Friday. Next week I'm flying out to Portugal to run a workshop... it's a hard life.'

He handed me his business card. 'Silver Fox – Senior Consultant – BS Consulting.' 'Lean is about making life easier,' it stated on the back of the card.

'I thought you did well today,' he said to me. 'You would make a good consultant. If you ever fancy a chat... give me a call.'

'By the way, what does BS stand for?' I asked.

'Bull Shit Consulting,' he said stony-faced. Then he smirked, 'No, that was just a bad consultant joke. It stands for Blue Sky... Blue Sky Consulting.'

We both looked up. It sounded optimistic, considering it rained for well over 360 days of the year in Wales!

I shook his hand firmly. As he drove away I waved at him like I would wave at a relative leaving my house at Christmas. Back in the factory I hoped things had cooled down. They hadn't. They had got worse. The paint plant had broken down again, production was way behind target and the union reps wanted to discuss why there was no overtime this weekend.

I sat in my office with the door closed. I fiddled with the guy's business card. His words spinning around in my head, *You would make a good consultant... give me a call.*

I closed my eyes and pictured myself as a footloose and fancy-free consultant wandering about the business world leaving advice on people's pillows like the Milk Tray man from the adverts. That was it, my mind was made up. I was going to become a business consultant if it was the last thing I ever did. Not to sound too desperate, I decided to give it a week or two before I called him.

Much later that night, when driving home, I stopped off at Asda to check out what briefcases they had in stock. I even bought myself a pair of cream chinos.

3

My First Sighting of Sushi

IT WAS VERY unprofessional I know, but I couldn't help myself. After another disastrous start at the factory, I called The Silver Fox up before midday the very next morning.

'Giz a job,' I more or less begged.

An interview got arranged. Two weeks after that, I handed my notice in at the steering column company. Bruce called me a two-faced, useless cunt. I didn't take it personally. Bruce called everyone a two-faced, useless cunt, even the handicapped woman with the funny shaped arms who worked on the presses.

I felt so excited. I couldn't wait to tell people what I was going to be. Only problem was, I didn't really know what I was actually going to be. More importantly, I really didn't know if I would be any good at whatever it was I was going to be. Could I do what The Silver Fox had done in my company? Did I have the intellect and the balls to control someone like Mad Bruce? Was I more sheep than sheepdog? The doubts crept in.

'Also, you will need to set up your own business and become self-employed,' The Silver Fox told me after I had accepted the role.

'Hang on, hang on, what do you mean set up my own business and become... self... self... self-employed?' I stuttered.

Although most of the consultants worked one hundred per cent for **BS Consulting**, they were all registered as one-man operations. The bottom line was, it was a much better way of not paying so much tax, he added.

I sat on the edge of my bed, mouth open in shock. He may as well have told me I needed to put a goldfish bowl on my head and fly to space. Where would I start? What would I need to do? What would I call my business? 'The Useless Dick Corporation,' sprang to mind.

I wondered if there was anyone I could talk to. The only self-employed people I knew consisted of a cowboy builder (who was actually a builder and a pretend cowboy on weekends), a reasonably successful drug dealer, and a man who rushed around the town collecting pools money while avoiding muggers!

'Nothing to it,' my cowboy builder told me, 'just get a good accountant.'

'What about your accountant?' I asked.

He laughed, 'A good one, I said.'

Where the hell would I find an accountant? None of my friends or family had every needed one. Defence lawyers, yes, but that's a completely different book.

And it wasn't like I could type 'compare-the-accountant-supermarket.com' into Google. It didn't exist in those days. Eventually, I tracked one down living in a damp room above an old ale-house in foggy London town. Fagan was his name and he lived with the Artful Dodger and Oliver Twist. That's a lie. His name was Derek, a straight-talking wise-guy with a head for figures and ice-blue hitman eyes, from Pontypridd.

His advice was plain and simple.

'Always keep your records up to date.'

'Don't fiddle... that's my job,' he joked. (I think he joked.)

'And never fuck about behind your wife's back, especially with your next door neighbour.' I looked at him. 'Long story, never mind.' He then proceeded to talk for two hours about fighting, drinking, golfing, shagging and his three divorces. It was then I understood the last piece of advice.

Before handing me a bill for £100, he also suggested not to waste my money on buying a new car. 'Contract hire one on a three-year lease instead,' he said. 'With the amount of miles you will be doing, just think of a car as a tool of the job, just like a phone. We'll claim it against tax.'

Like a complete village idiot, I didn't know anything about VAT and tax. I didn't even know they were different things. I was hesitant, but decided to take his advice about the car

'You're doing what?' My old man stopped reading the *Daily Mirror*.

I explained again about leasing the car.

'But then after three years you keep it, don't you?' he grunted.

'No, Dad, I give it back.'

'You give it back? Have you been smoking that wacky baccy?' he looked at me as if I had finally tipped over the edge.

'Yes, Dad, no, Dad... I'll get another new one.'

It reminded me of Peter Kay's garlic bread sketch about the first time his old man went to Spain and discovered garlic bread. All through the holiday he would look at the waiter and say, 'Garlic... bread?!'

My Dad's catchphrase was similar. 'Lease... car?!' For days he would phone me up all worried like. 'Tell me again, son... you get the car, you pay for it and then you give it back. Are you sure?'

'Don't worry, Dad... I know what I'm doing.'

In truth, I didn't know what the hell I was doing, but it felt exciting. Overnight I became a bandit, a desperado, a rebel without a clue!

And at least I had a brand-new car for the first time in my life to drive around in. I went for a silver Picasso. Not the most upmarket car in the world, but I didn't want anything too flash. The Silver Fox had warned me BS Consulting frowned on its consultants turning up to clients in big flash cars.

'Gives out the wrong message,' he said.

That suited me. I'd never really been a car-type of person. As long as it had a good CD player and I didn't have to jump-start it down a hill, I didn't care.

I reckoned the kitchen table would do as my very own office, until my wife put a stop to that. 'Either it's the small box room, the garage or your mother's,' she strongly advised.

Three hours and a string of swear words later I eventually assembled the computer desk from Ikea in the tiny box room. I bought a cork board, like the ones found in kitchens, to stick all the important messages I would soon been having on it. I couldn't work out how to nail it to a plasterboard wall, so I hung it with lumps of Blu Tack instead. It kept falling down at odd times of the night and scaring the life out of all of us. In the end my wife threw it in the bin!

Now I was ready to enter the kingdom of consultancy.

Self-employed – check

Own company – check

Own office (with wardrobes) – check

New car – check

Chinos – check

Bath – check

My big first day coincided with a business get-together. The Business Review was a day when everyone in the business got together to look at the last three months' performance and discuss future developments.

'It will be a great way to meet everyone,' The Silver Fox informed me. 'Sadly, I'm going on holidays, so I won't be there... but you will be fine.'

Getting out of my car and walking to the conference centre I felt as if I was walking into primary school on my first day. At least this time my mother wasn't by my side trying to wipe stale Ready Brek off my face with a hankie covered in her own spit.

I didn't know what to expect or what I would do. What if I said something wrong? What if I tripped over when I walked in? What if I shat myself? Oh no, what if I did? Shat myself right there in front of the whole class. No, not the class, whatever one called a pack, or a stack, or a brain-cell of consultants. I hadn't actually pooped in my pants since that first day in primary school. But the kids, and the teachers, the bastards, never let me forget it.

Nervously, I hung around at the back of the room in my new

chinos with my arse cheeks clenched tightly together, just in case. I even had new socks and underpants on. To this day, I still don't know why I made my wife iron them. Perhaps I thought I would have to go through some kind of initiation ceremony similar to the ones on rugby tours. In my mind, I convinced myself a brain-cell of power-crazed consultants were going to grab me, bend me over a desk and ram a cucumber (or maybe a pack of whiteboard markers) up my nether regions.

That would definitely not be the moment to shit oneself.

After glancing around the room, I quickly came to the conclusion that the fifteen or so white, middle-aged guys, holding cups of coffee as if their lives depended on it, weren't the 'ramming a cucumber up my nether regions' type. They seemed quite normal in an intellectual sort of way. One looked like a trainspotter; a few looked like supply teachers with arm patches on their jackets. One reminded me of a Conservative MP. Then there was one shifty-looking character, in the tightest fitting chinos, who looked more like an old 1970s porn star than a consultant. I could even hear the porn music playing in the background as I stared at him. I wondered what his porn star name was. Todd Ball-Bags, I assumed.

'Oh, shit,' I muttered as someone saw me giggling to myself.

A mountain of a man, as wide as he was tall, wandered towards me. 'I'm Tom… You must be Anthony.' He shook my hand firmly.

Others soon came over and introduced themselves. I'm useless with names and forgot them straight away, except for Todd Ball-Bags. They cracked a couple of in-jokes, which I didn't understand but laughed at anyway. I began to relax a little.

Next, in trotted a gaggle of office girls. Again, smartly dressed, very efficient-looking with a hint of sophistication. Sophisticated in the sense they didn't smell of Players No. 6, cheap perfume and false tan. Definitely not Valley girls. Must be from Cardiff, I imagined.

Two minutes to nine, everyone grabbed a quick refill, and sat down around the large U-shaped formation of tables. Tom motioned me to sit next to him. I did as I was told. I pushed my brand-new briefcase containing a few pens, a ruler, two tubes of Tipp-ex, a calculator, a stapler which was bigger than my shoe and writing pad under the table out of harm's way.

In each corner of the room a flip chart stood waiting to be filled in with important stuff. I waited nervously. More laughing and slurping of coffee followed.

All of a sudden the main door opened. In sauntered the four partners of the business. The head honchos wandered in like the suited and booted gangsters from the famous scene in the movie *Reservoir Dogs*.

The Glass Is Always Half Full partner, The 5-Star Gimp, The Master and The Prof.

Everything went deadly quiet. It was as if four headmasters had entered the room carrying brand new canes covered in six-inch nails.

The Glass Is Always Half Full partner unashamedly bounced towards me like a highly-strung Mexican jumping bean.

'You must be Anthony?' he almost yelled out his question. 'Glad you're on board.' Even accounting for his large mop of ginger hair, he seemed to be an extremely outgoing and infectious individual.

With my cheeks glowing red, I shyly nodded in his direction. He plonked himself down near the front, a gigantic, positive grin on his thirty-five-year-old smooth baby features.

The Master sat three chairs away from me. I slyly spied him out of the corner of my eye. He looked a different beast altogether from ginger top. A deadly serious-looking, been-through-the-mill, fifty-six year old, with a hint of a Bobby Charlton wrap-over hairstyle taking place on top. Small in size, yet one of those people I assumed gained respect without looking for it.

From researching the BS Consulting website before joining, I'd discovered The Master had started the business six years before. Within that time it had grown from a one-man operation to a fairly big consultancy business of nearly twenty-five staff. (Well, all self-employed staff.)

He didn't really acknowledge me. He didn't really acknowledge anyone. He sat deep in thought like a doctor about to give someone bad news about a failed operation. I looked away before he spied me.

Out of everyone in the room, including the nerdy Trainspotter, The Prof looked the least impressive. On saying that, he came to the table with the most impressive credentials. A highly-decorated academic, yet still someone who, in my basic opinion, looked like they would be the last person to get picked to play football in the school yard. And then be made to go in goals.

With his thick bottle-top glasses and mismatched clothes, I figured whatever he was a professor in, it certainly wasn't in how to dress. I'm no fashion guru (unless wearing faded jeans and a black T-shirt for the last thirty years can be classed as the height of fashion), but even I could see he had less dress-sense than that old, weird *Doctor Who* bloke with the long scarf.

'He's a professor of Lean Thinking,' Tom informed me during a quick coffee break.

'Oh,' I muttered.

'He's got degrees in it, and letters after his name. He's one of the best Lean Thinkers in the country.'

I wanted to ask, did being a Lean Thinker mean he didn't have to do a lot of it? But I was new and I didn't want to get off on the wrong foot, especially with someone who had letters after their name. I wondered what The Prof's careers officer had said when he told him what he wanted to be instead of a priest!

However on that first morning, I didn't care about his lack of style. As he stood at the front talking, every word floating out of his mouth came alive. I didn't understand most of what he was on about. In fact, I wondered if it was actually English. But it sounded clever, sounded important. He instantly became my very own *Wizard of Oz*; my brains from *Here Come the Double Deckers*. A man who could easily outsmart the un-outsmartable Stephen Hawking if they appeared against each other on the TV show *Blockbusters*. Although I reckon, the wheelchair guru would have probably beaten The Prof in a one-on-one foot race.

Nevertheless, it was the partner with the little round glasses and the extraordinary imposing moustache standing next to him who fascinated me most of all. Apparently, he was the strategic expert for the business (the partner that is, not his moustache). On first impression he reminded me of a First World War general who I also imagined ran a kinky S&M club somewhere near Milton Keynes in his spare time. In truth, I never found out what he did in his spare time. But even up to the day I finished with the business, I couldn't look at The 5-Star Gimp without picturing him sitting on a red velvet throne in black Speedos, twirling his moustache, while some large buxom breasted woman whipped some businessman dressed in a gimp mask and suspenders.

A rather aloof individual, he prided himself on rubbing shoulders with kings, dictators, and leaders of British industry. Individuals with huge egos, posh cars and, I guess, small penises. I got the impression he didn't like bothering with commoners like us.

On that morning his message to everyone in the room was simple. 'The business needs to grow or the business will die,' he yelled. 'We need to be number one, and destroy the competition.' Bolt upright, he marched about the front of the room with his right arm raised in the air to indicate growth. Bizarrely, to me it looked more like some kind of Nazi salute.

'Fuck me,' I thought, 'I've been here less than an hour and already some part-time perverted general wants me to go goose-stepping to London and beat up all the other consultants working for KPMG.'

I actually sniggered to myself. I couldn't help it. I've never been one to take life seriously. Even at funerals I am always thinking of something funny that could happen. The sound of a phone ringing from inside the coffin, or the altar boy accidentally setting the priest's robe on fire, then having to throw holy water over him. It's just the way I'm wired. I'm still not sure if it's been a strength or weakness of mine over the years!

For the rest of that morning I tried to concentrate on what the partners were saying. They talked about growth and markets and products and margins and competition and money and utilisation and European travel and UK funding. My head spun.

I nodded politely and wrote stuff down on my pad to pretend I knew what the hell they were going on about. They threw words about I hadn't even heard of. You think spending three years achieving a master's degree with the Open University would have helped me a little bit. But not a bloody hope. I cursed myself for not studying more and just being happy to join the Forty Per Cent Club. This was a bit like the Breakfast Club but with a bunch of much lazier and weirder bastards. I became a member after discovering I only needed an overall mark of forty per cent to pass. Who needed distinctions and special awards?

At about eleven o'clock the main door creaked opened. A consultant entered and quietly took a seat at the other end of the table from me. He looked different to the others, scruffier. His bushy hair stuck up like he hadn't been to bed for a month and his clothes weren't ironed. 'Sorry I'm late,' he said in a posh English accent, 'my partner's gone to join the circus today.'

No one batted an eyebrow. The Prof carried on talking.

'Hang on a cotton-picking minute.' Yet again, my mind cartwheeled out of control. 'What does he mean, *My partner's gone to join the circus today?*' Firstly, was his partner a man, woman, or some kind of big hairy beast? Was his partner a midget who got fired from a large cannon every night? Or a lion tamer? Or the bearded lady... what the fuck did he mean?

Tom must have sensed my confusion. 'She's a cook,' he

whispered. 'She does stints with the travelling circus around the country.'

'Thanks,' I muttered. I then wanted to know if it was a proper circus or one of those freak show ones. My mind drifted away from what The Prof was saying as I pictured the woman handing out a plate of egg and chips to the Elephant Man.

'Do you want salt and vinegar on it, John?'

'Noooooooooooooooooooooooooo,' the poor deformed man replied while whacking on the tomato sauce.

I smiled. I was going to really like it here.

Thankfully, my head got a well-earned rest as we stopped for lunch. Well that was until I saw all the strange food spread out on the table. Plates of sushi, salad sandwiches and carrot-filled vol-au-vents stared up at me. To be honest, I had never seen sushi before, never mind tasted it. Where I came from people got beaten up if they offered someone a sandwich without any ham or chicken in it. And fish needed to be coated in half a ton of greasy batter before any of my family and friends would consider putting it in their mouths. I watched The Prof fill up his plate with the non-meat items.

Interesting!

I stuck to a few sausage rolls and some crisps. In the bog I sat contemplating my first morning. It had been such a different experience to anything I had ever been involved with previously. I had met the partners, seen sushi for the first time and sat close to a bloke who had a partner who knew circus folk.

I marvelled at what the second half would bring. Maybe a team-building exercise to make a Trojan horse out of Post-it notes or maybe they'd have us cut up a rat like we did in general science. I didn't know if there would be any link between cutting up a rodent and being a consultant, but who cared; it was one of those crazy kinds of days.

Although many bizarre thoughts spun like battling tops around my mind, I didn't for one minute expect to see what I actually saw when I re-entered the room. There, in the corner, on an exercise bike sat a bloke called Mike. I kid you not. Mike on a Bike. Honestly, I thought my sausage rolls had been spiked with acid. He sat dressed in full Lycra training gear including a blue headband. He looked like a deranged tortoise from those *Wallace and Gromit*-style adverts.

The Glass Is Always Half Full partner bounced about next to him. 'Sit down everyone... You will love this,' he grinned.

I looked at Tom. He rolled his eyes.

When everyone was in position, Mike on the Bike began pedalling away, like an amphetamine-fuelled hamster. Every now and again The Glass Is Always Half Full partner checked Mike's pulse and speed, and then loudly gave him instructions.

Mike puffed and panted away. His face got redder and redder with each kilometre pedalled. At one stage I thought he was going to faint, or better still, keel over and die. Now that would have been a weird start to my new career, but one hell of a dramatic addition to this book. Alas, he didn't.

After ten minutes he stopped. The Glass Is Always Half Full partner clapped his hands. 'Right, what do you think that meant?'

'He's training for the Tour de France?' was my first thought. But I kept my thoughts to myself.

'He's unfit,' someone replied.

Everyone laughed.

'He's a cunt,' I heard Tom muttering to someone called Joe.

I burst out laughing. Everyone stopped and stared at me. I slumped down in my chair.

Evidently, it had something to do with the need to give a business regular health checks. Everyone nodded in agreement, even the office girls. I thought I'd better do the same. I rubbed my chin for extra effect.

Near the end, we got spilt into small teams and asked to discuss what direction we wanted the business to go in the next few years. Then, oddly, we were asked what we as individuals wanted out of the business. I was more used to companies telling the employees what they wanted and the employees fitting in around those plans. This was so very different.

Individuals in my team talked about wanting to retire by the time they got to the age of fifty. Fucking hell, retire at fifty! The job I had beforehand I would have been lucky to still be alive at that age. Others said they wanted to work abroad more. One, older, consultant said he wanted to open a café in west Wales. I chuckled. No one else did. They looked at me again. I went bright red again. I had to learn to control my outbursts.

'I would like to do something with adverts,' I quietly muttered.

'Great,' The Glass Is Always Half Full partner overheard me and butted in. 'You can help with our marketing literature.'

'Arrrggghh... fucking sit on that careers officer,' I said to myself. 'You told me I couldn't do adverts and now I'm helping out with some marketing literature.' I didn't know exactly what marketing literature was, but it sounded important.

The entire day proved to be like a breath of fresh air. I felt like I had risen from the dead and was now walking through the streets of Damascus on a donkey with strange-looking people with patches on their jackets following me about, waving palms and trying to touch my hair.

They finished the day by flashing up on the overhead projector the set of values the business prided itself on being. They all sat there mouthing the words. The values reminded me of the rules Snowball the Pig made up after the animals in *Animal Farm* chased the humans off the farm. They went something like:

1. No consultant shall wear fancy suits and expensive watches.

2. No consultant shall drive posh, flash cars.

3. No consultant shall drink alcohol on a school night.

4. No consultant shall bad-mouth any other partner or work colleague.

5. All consultants are equal.

Even though I found it slightly *Stepford Wives* creepy, I was more than happy to sign up to all of these values. I liked the fact there didn't seem to be any internal politics like I had been used to in other companies I'd worked for. Also it was good to see the business wasn't packed with a bunch of slimy alligators in crocodile shoes talking bullshit and driving top of the range cars. Even the partners looked more like 'posher' gypsies trying to flog cheap carpets or pave people's drives, than being the leading minds of industry. I liked the down-to-earth look. It suited me.

When the business review ended, I couldn't wait to get home and tell everyone how my day had gone. I'm not really a person who revels in talking about work, good day or bad day. I never tried to bore anyone with the boring job I did. I realise that must sound odd as you sit there reading this, but I don't. Just like the Beautiful South song, I too, like to keep it all in. However I burst through my front door, as if I had just seen Elvis Presley filling up his car in the petrol station.

My family thought I had been abducted by aliens and given a personality transplant. They couldn't shut me up. I told them all about The Master, the happy Glass Is Always Full partner, The Prof and The 5-Star Gimp (I didn't go into great detail concerning his S&M tendencies). The consultant whose partner owned Billy Smart's circus! I explained about sushi and sandwiches with no meat in them. (They didn't believe me!) I drew a picture of what it looked like. I told them how I had got to write on the flip chart. I didn't tell them I spelt a few words wrong. I didn't dare tell them about our values, they were top secret.

'I fancy going veggie like The Prof,' I announced. Maybe eating only onions, tomatoes and salads, would make me a Lean Thinker too. I gave my pork chop to the dog.

My non-meat existence lasted an entire hour before I sneaked into the fridge and ate a pack of cheap cooked ham, a scotch egg and three BBQ chicken wings.

4

Bathing with the Fishes!

IF ANNE FRANK had been a consultant, the entry in her diary about the first two weeks into her new job would have gone something like this.

'Dear Diary, I've sat in the office for long periods, not doing much. Drunk lots of strong coffee, and ate lots of lots of Greggs pasties. I liked the chicken ones the best. Still don't understand what the hell a consultant really does. But I'm having a great time, and not a Nazi in sight. (Although The 5-Star Gimp did pop in wearing jackboots and twirling anal love beads in his hands.)'

Back in my 'real' world, Tom took me under his large wing. He explained all about what I would be doing over the coming months to start earning revenue for the business. He explained how consultants only made money when they were 'client facing'. Getting trained up, or out shadowing a consultant (shadowing is when a fresh 'fish' sits in the room and makes notes while watching an old 'shark' strut his stuff), doesn't put money in the cookie jar.

'The first few months are the hardest,' he warned me. 'But it will get easier when you start getting your own regular customers.'

'A bit like being a prostitute,' I smiled.

'What?'

'The sooner I get my own clients the less I will have to stand on street corners waiting for weird men in cars to slow down.'

I didn't think he appreciated the vivid picture I painted. But it made sense to me. From that moment on my aim was to become a high-class consultant hooker as quickly as possible, having strawberries and champagne fed to me by Richard Gere, instead of being like some old streetwalker in hot pants getting into a car with some old pervert in a raincoat.

My new business was split into two sections. One half worked mainly in Wales with funding from the Welsh Office. The other, 'posher', branch of BS Consulting dealt with large, worldwide, corporate clients. Some of the biggest companies in the world appeared on our portfolio. That's where I wanted to be. In the 'Pretty Woman meets Richard Gere' world. I knew to get there I first needed to earn my stripes.

By the end of my second week, there was only so much hanging about, drinking coffee and eating stodgy food I could take. Thankfully, the following week I got the opportunity to shadow a workshop in a well-known confectionery company in darkest England.

That Monday morning I couldn't wait to get there. The M4, formerly known as a car park, did make me wait a bit longer than I appreciated. (One of the many curses of life on the road for a hardcore consultant.)

When I arrived thirty minutes late, I nervously signed in and received my visitor's badge.

"Anthony Bunko – Consultant – BS Consulting."

It almost brought a tear to my eye. I still have that badge somewhere in a drawer along with a football medal from my primary school and a photo of myself and my mate Sully when we were ten watching the wrestling in Minehead Butlin's.

Walking through the main office I thought I'd entered the wonderful world of Disney. Everything appeared technicoloured, almost picture perfect. All that was missing was Mickey Mouse, the magic kingdom and gangs of lard-arsed Americans waddling about in gigantic jeans while wolfing down enormous hot dogs.

Arty posters lined the walls; colourful, modern furniture dotted everywhere. It held me spellbound. I glided about, mouth wide open, eyes large as saucers. I couldn't get over how young and attractive everyone appeared. Smartly dressed women and men everywhere I looked. The average age I guess must have been about twenty-three. I didn't see anyone with grey hair, not even a strand, or a wrinkle! Maybe it was Disney, and I had accidently been transported onto the 'It's a small world' ride. Everyone seemed so polite which felt so unnatural to me. Don't forget, I had spent most of my working life surviving in the trenches of the Welsh Valleys fighting against overweight, sweaty, businessmen kitted out in one hundred per cent nylon suits from Burton's, cheap ties and classic white socks.

This was so, so much different.

It got worse, or should I say, weirder.

I passed a big, round, yellow table. Six twenty-somethings, with perfect teeth and skin, sat around it. I stopped dead in amazement. With serious looks on their young faces, they sampled different coloured chocolate sweets from a huge bowl and then discussed each one in great detail.

'Fuck me sideways with a rusty poker,' I thought. 'What a brilliant way to spend any morning of the week, never mind a cold, grey Monday morning.' I imagined what my old grandfather, an ex-miner with a working-class mindset and piles the size of blood oranges, would have said if I came home and told him, 'Hey, Gramp, I've had a hard day in the office today. I had to eat 163 green sweets and then write an essay about them.'

He would have kicked me in the balls, and whacked me with the shovel he kept under the bed.

Still shaking my head in disbelief, I finally reached the training room. There, sixteen people, mostly good-looking women, sat around the table.

'Thank you, God.' I looked up to the heavens and made a sly sign of the cross.

Full of energy, The Silver Fox (the old 'shark') stood at the front of the room. He explained briefly who I was and why I was there. No one really looked at me. In their eyes I was a nobody. I was a fresh fish.

The team had already spent the previous week carrying

out a diagnostic assessment of a section of the business. A diagnostic assessment is a simple method (made a lot more complicated by consultants for obvious reasons) where the team would investigate each step of a process to highlight any major issues.

'The aim,' The Silver Fox whispered to me during a break, 'without us appearing too smug, is to get them to see how crap they are, and then, without appearing even smugger, get them to get us to help them fix their problems.'

I had heard the saying, 'Consultants will borrow someone's watch and then tell them the time... but at a cost.' The Silver Fox proved to be one of the best watch-borrowing, time-telling individuals I had ever seen. He had the people in the room throwing their trendy Swatches at him in droves.

'Right,' he told the group, 'now the easy part. You need to come up with suggestions on what you need to do to improve your processes.' He was quite precise with his use of words.

He winked at me. Pound signs rolled about in his eyes.

He let the group brainstorm possible ways to make things better. They talked and talked and talked. They analysed everything in minute detail. They discussed and discussed and argued and argued. Everyone had to have a say. Everyone had an opinion, their very own, unique opinion. One bloke suggested something completely different to the rest of them. I'm positive he had nothing to do with the session and he had accidentally wandered into the meeting by mistake. I'm sure he was the cleaner or had just turned up to fix the waterpipes and then just got involved.

I sat listening to them go on and on for hours. Although they were really smart people with minds the size of a planet, and used words longer than most of my sentences, they couldn't decide on anything. I soon came to the conclusion they were all completely bonkers.

On my life, if these people had been on the jury in the Yorkshire Ripper murder case and the prosecutor had submitted CCTV evidence of the murderer in full view whacking the prostitutes to a pulp, plus if Sutcliffe himself had stood up in the dock and yelled out, 'Yes, your honour, I did it and here is the lump hammer,' while pulling the murder weapon out of his stained underpants, these people would still have taken six months to come up with their verdict. And then I'm not sure they would have found him guilty.

Even The Silver Fox struggled to get them to 'think outside the box' (one of the favourite bullshit statements I soon used regularly). I thought, 'Fuck, if he's struggling, how the hell am I going to cope when it's my turn to step into this arena?' It would be like getting fed to the lions.

I suddenly felt vulnerable and scared.

Instead of commuting back and forth every day for that week, I stayed in a fine, stately-home-slash-hotel, housed in thirty acres of its own grounds. My bedroom was located right at the top of the main building. Mine was the only bedroom up on the top floor. The rest of the upper floor was taken up with offices.

It was great though, very quiet, with fantastic views of the gardens. The only disadvantage was it didn't have its own bathroom, only a sink. I've always liked relaxing in a bath. But it wasn't the end of the world, a few doors down was a huge bathroom with a big, old-fashioned china bath. And, since all the office staff finished at five, there was no one else around!

After a run through the woods, where I nearly got savaged by an Alsatian dog who thought I was about to attack its female owner, I needed a bath. With just a towel around my waist I tiptoed in and ran the water. Just before stepping in I noticed there wasn't any shower gel or shampoo. I raced back to my room to get some, but, I hadn't brought anything with me. Above the sink was a dispenser of clean, white gel hand-wash.

'That will do,' I thought.

I found a plastic cup and squirted a few shots into it. The liquid went all over my fingers and down the side of the see-through plastic container.

Still with the towel around my waist, I skipped out of the room. I stopped dead in my tracks like a rabbit caught in the headlights of a car. Two cleaning ladies, Hoovers in hands, stared at me. The three of us stood in the corridor in silence. We all looked at the cup at the same time. I could tell straight away what they were thinking. 'Oh look, Doris, it's a weird bloke sneaking around the corridors wrapped in a towel, holding a cup of man-juice which he has obviously just jacked off into.'

They nudged each other in a 'we know what you've been doing, you dirty Welsh bastard' sort of way that only cleaners are allowed to do. Before I could explain they walked off giggling.

I rushed into the bathroom, bright red. I threw the cup on the floor in disgust as if it actually *was* spunk in the plastic cup. Part of me wanted to chase after them and tell them it was shower gel not love froth. I considered leaving them a quick note to explain. The more evil part of me wished I had filled the entire plastic cup to the brim with the spunky-looking substance. Now that would have given them something to talk about during their cleaners' coffee break.

'Good gosh,' I imagined one of them telling the others while breaking a Kit-Kat in half, 'that bloke in room thirteen must have bollocks like a prize bull. The seediest ball bag I've ever seen.'

I didn't write the note. Let's just say I tried my best to avoid them for the rest of my life. But, sadly, I kept bumping into them wherever I went. I'm sure they followed me around on purpose. I even saw them in the fish aisle at Sainsbury's!

In the end I thought, 'Oh fuck it, if I want to toss off into a plastic cup, why can't I?' How weird was that? I was suddenly boasting about something I hadn't even done.

To make matters worse, two days later, I ended up flooding the same bathroom. This time I'd gone out and bought my own shower gel. I rushed into the bathroom to run the water. My phone rang in the other room. Tom called to see how everything was going. We had a good chat but by the time I'd got off the phone about twenty minutes later, to my horror, I found the bathroom almost submerged.

I panicked. I waded through the four inches of water and switched off the taps. I sank to my knees and began scooping the water up with my hands. Suddenly, there was a knock on my door. I opened it. The concierge and a gang of his staff rushed in like firemen. My spillage had seeped into various rooms below. With hands full of towels and a water-sucker thing they cleaned it all up. They didn't say anything, just glared at me in an 'and you are supposed to be the consultant' sort of way, as they trooped back out.

I'd been there less than a week (my first real week as a consultant) and already the cleaners thought I was some kind of perverted, spunk monster, while in the concierge's mind, I was an irresponsible, spoilt, consultant brat. I didn't know which was worse.

On the last day of the workshop, I entered the training room to find a black box device located in the middle of the main table. It looked like a starfighter spaceship from the *Star Wars* movies. I hadn't noticed it before.

'Jenny Jackson wants to be part of today's discussion,' one of the leaders mentioned casually.

I looked around the table. There didn't seem to be anyone new there. Where was Jenny then? I thought, 'Fashionably late, I bet.'

How wrong could I have been?

Jenny, I soon discovered, was in fact sitting in America staring at her own black starfighter spaceship from the *Star Wars* movies device thing. She aimed to communicate with the group from five thousand miles away. I thought it was a joke at first. Looking back now, I realise I must have been so technologically backwards, I may as well have been sat on a bridge, cross-eyed, plucking on an old banjo. But, at the time, I had never seen anything like that before, except in *Red Dwarf*.

Someone switched on the box.

A soft cough sound preceded the words, 'Hi, everyone, I'm Jenny with the big, black box.' OK, I'm exaggerating, she just said, 'Hi, everyone, I'm Jenny,' but my mind may have added a word or two on for sexual effect.

'Hi, Jenny,' everyone in turn replied.

It was 4 a.m. in New York and with one switch Jenny was now part of our team, part of the discussion. Another voice to add to all the other voices talking, discussing and arguing. However, as the morning progressed, Jenny seemed to definitely be the most sensible and decisive one there – and she wasn't even there!

After a while I got bored with just sitting at the back, listening. My mind started to wander and ask more fundamental questions about the lady across the Pond. What did she look like? Was she fat or thin? Did she have a face for the radio? Did she have a gammy eye? Did she have any eyes at all? Maybe she was just a head, with tubes coming out of the top. Maybe she was the black box? Was she wearing pyjamas or in the buff? What was she doing when all the talking went on? I assumed she was a very professional individual sitting in the study in her house, listening. Yet somewhere in my mind I made up images of her doing mundane tasks as she listened. Doing the washing-up with the box balanced on the draining board. Sitting on the toilet with her hand over her black box so we couldn't hear her peeing? Walking around Walmart with the device in the shopping trolley?

I know it was childish and immature of me. But, however hard I tried, the situation just tickled my funny bone.

When the workshop was all over, Anne Frank, the consultant, wrote:

'Dear Diary, I had my first, chocolate-coated taste of shadowing this week. Very interesting, a bit slow at times but a real eye-opener. By the way, don't mention the hotel bathroom.'

Even with its faults it was still miles better than the world I had come from. I now reaised that a big part of my new role would be learning to listen to strange people talking bollocks instead of getting things done.

When I was leaving, one of the group leaders handed me a huge bag of goodies consisting of products the company had launched but couldn't sell. All kinds of stuff I couldn't buy at the garage in Dowlais Top.

As I watched my daughter work her way through her fourth chocolate bar I thought, 'Forget the mishaps and bullshit, this job is perfect for me. And I'm perfect for this job.'

Then my world came tumbling down as I got introduced to The Mincer.

5

The Mincer

EVEN WRITING THE words 'The Mincer' still makes my blood run cold and my entire body to break out in goose-bumps. Before BS Consulting the word 'mincer' simply conjured up an image of bloodied meat getting squeezed from the end of a sausage machine. Now, every time I hear it, I picture grown men standing, ashen-faced, shaking and being totally humiliated.

And the partner known simply as The Master was the reason why. Deep down, I don't think he meant to be a sadistic, heartless, vicious bastard, who, in his day, would have made Idi Amin look like a fresh-faced *Blue Peter* presenter. He just held such high standards. And since he started the business he expected everyone to abide by these high standards. No matter what it took or how many consultants he upset, killed, or maimed in the process.

I'd been in the business for over a month and hadn't earned a dime for my supper. Not a bad life, considering I was getting paid more money than I had ever earned in any of my previous jobs. Nonetheless, I wanted to be hitting some kind of revenue target. When I wasn't contributing to the fund pot I felt a bit of a sponger, waiting for the Giro cheque to pop through the letterbox on a Wednesday so I could dash down to Wetherspoon's and spend it all.

In my mind, I knew the sooner I got some pound signs against my name the better I would feel.

One morning I sat in the office with Tom and Joe. The phone rang. Zoe the secretary informed us The Master wanted someone to help him run a two-day workshop in mid-Wales. A paid assignment.

Here was my chance to get my name on the board. Being rather green, I didn't notice Tom and Joe purposely keeping their heads down low.

'I'll do it,' I excitedly replied.

Both men turned and looked at me. Tom smirked.

Joe puffed out his cheeks. 'Good luck,' he jokingly made the sign of the cross.

'Welcome to *The Mincer*,' Tom's words seem to shiver as they slipped out of his mouth.

'What?'

'You'll find out.'

'Tom,' Zoe cried from across the office. She smiled at me. 'Don't listen to them, Anthony, they are only winding you up. The Master isn't an ogre.' She may have been slightly biased since The Master was her father. I did notice she didn't look me in the eye. But I didn't care. If I could cope with Bruce McFuckin' Nutcase, my ex-MD, I could cope with anyone.

Bright and early the next morning I nervously walked into the office. The Master sat in the corner with his head down, writing.

'Morning, Master,' I said. Of course I didn't say Master; that would have been really weird.

Silence greeted me.

Maybe he hadn't heard me. I repeated my greeting but a little louder. Again, nothing. Was he ignoring me? Had he gone deaf? Maybe he was dead. No, I could see his fingers moving.

I sat down in the opposite corner, worrying whether I had done something wrong. I pretended to do some work. He grunted and groaned to himself. Ten minutes later, he stood up abruptly. 'Hi, Anthony. Come on, let's go.'

We travelled to the venue in his car. He didn't do small talk. He only said what he needed to say. 'The company makes air conditioning units all over the world. We are meeting with the senior management team to discuss opening up possible new markets to maximise their sales.'

My role, he explained clearly and concisely, was to man the flip chart and fuck all else.

I nodded and grinned like a village idiot.

Ten businessmen and The Master sat around the huge boardroom table. I stood waiting by the flip chart, marker pen in hand.

Before I clarify what happened next, let me explain the reasons why it proved to be a disaster waiting to happen. First off, I didn't know anything about marketing, and nothing about their business. I really didn't understand the BS Consulting approach to consulting. And I'm not sure if I had mentioned this before, but I'm not the best speller in the world, especially when I had eleven sets of eyes watching me. Then there was The Master himself.

So here goes.

The session started off pleasantly enough. The Master opened up the debate by throwing questions around like plates at a Greek wedding. The conversation bounced around the table several times for about ten minutes. To me it sounded like a foreign language. I stood there, fascinated, soaking up the atmosphere. Then the spotlight of doom unexpectedly shone on me.

'Right... that's a very good point,' The Master said to one of the guys. He then shouted out, 'Anthony, write that down.'

'Write what down?' I thought. 'Which part?' Everyone stared at me. I stood rigid like a frightened chicken that had accidently walked into KFC.

The Master's head spun right around, similar to the girl off *The Exorcist*. His eyes burnt into my skin. 'I said, Write it down.' Everyone in the room looked embarrassed for me. Panic smacked me in the face; terror grabbed my exposed balls and squeezed tightly.

'Which part?' my voice shook, my armpits soaking wet.

'The main points... you idiot!' he barked. He was right. I must have looked like the biggest village idiot in a 'biggest village idiot, *X Factor*-style' competition. He tutted and told me what to write.

He started talking to the group again.

I stood shell-shocked. I didn't know what to do. Should I listen then write down the main points? Or just write as much as I could? I panicked and didn't do either. Exactly the same thing happened a few minutes later. The Master growled at me like he was the nastiest pitbull dog in the world.

I decided to listen hard, and then write as much as I could. But my head was all over the place. I fucked up for the third time.

'I didn't say to write that,' The Master again belittled me in front of everyone.

I was thirty-seven years of age and, for the first time since my parents found a *Hustler* magazine under my bedroom carpet, I was getting a right royal bollocking. My shoulders slumped down, my legs wobbled. Even the other people in the room stared down at the table.

I decided my new strategy would be to just write as they discussed things. But I didn't know how to spell one of the words and by the time I figured out something which looked remotely like it, I missed the rest of the conversation. My brain refused to work. I went from a bad speller to the worst speller ever. I couldn't even spell Dick and Dora. I had a complete brain freeze.

A snarl replaced The Master's growl. I wondered if I could pretend to faint, or maybe fake a heart attack. Could I possibly dribble and say I had contracted rabies from my dog?

The more I concentrated on what they were saying, the more my head filled up with other weird stuff. Panic set in. Tom's words, 'Welcome to The Mincer,' floated around my brain. I could also see my dead career officer's face grinning at me. In his skeleton hands, he held out for me a miner's helmet and a pick.

I focused harder. No good. Whatever anyone around the table said just sounded like a noise to me. A blur of words mocked me with every syllable. The MD of the business either felt sorry for me or just needed to go out of the room so he could laugh his cock off. He called for a coffee break.

'Are you a fucking moron?' The Master stormed up to me and hissed, his face up close to mine. I stared at the floor. 'Get it fucking right and start listening! These people are paying good money for you.'

If truth be told, I wanted to headbutt The Master and run home. I filled up. He bounded off. I assumed to bite the head off a live bat. The rest of the session proved just as bad. In the end I only wrote on the flip chart like a doctor signing a prescription. It made no sense at all. God help the poor girl back in our office who had to turn the flip charts into a report. Hopefully, it would be Zoe's job. Serve her right for sending me into the lion's den in the first place.

At the end of the day, The Master and I sat in his car in stony silence. I was a broken man. Sweat and confidence drained from every pore in my body.

'Let's have a debrief on what happened today,' he said softly. 'How do you think it went?'

'You are a fucking psychopath who needs a good hammering,' I wanted to say but of course I didn't. 'I was terrible,' I muttered.

What I grew to like about The Master was, he never made things personal. He treated everyone equally as bad. 'No, you weren't terrible... you just need to listen and write what they say, when they say it.'

'I was trying, but I didn't know what they were on about and I can't spell and I'm a bit deaf in one ear and when I was seven my uncle ran away with a younger woman... and... and... and...' I made up every excuse I could think of.

I think he could sense my frustration and probably see the tears filling up in my eyes. We made a game plan for the second day which made me feel a little better. Problem was my wife and I had just had a new addition to the family. A baby girl named Georgia, who kept us up all that night. I hardly slept. The following morning I felt so tired, as well as feeling completely inadequate.

The next morning a white van nearly forcing The Master's brand new car off the road as we drove to the factory didn't put him in the best of moods. The van overtook us but pulled in suddenly when a car came the other way. The Master swerved to avoid contact and his car careered up a bank. The van sped off. Fuming like a raging bull, The Master chased after it with his horn blasting and the car lights flashing. At the next set of traffic lights The Master leapt out, raced up to the van and banged on the window. Two massive builders, twice his size, clambered out.

If I was truthful, part of me wanted him to get his teeth bashed in so the workshop would be cancelled. I didn't really want to get out of the car but reluctantly, I did. The Master stood poking the big guy in the chest. I sized the other one up. He looked like Desperate Dan's older and tougher-looking brother. He glared at me. My knees started to knock together. Luckily, or unluckily, the van driver apologised and we went on our way.

Again the workshop soon deteriorated into the same farce as the day before. Only I was actually even worse. I got more words wrong. I sweated like a rapist hiding in a Florida bush in a frogman's suit. The Master screamed at me in front of everyone even louder than the day before. It was the longest and most humiliating eight hours of my life. I felt like several lifetimes had rolled into one day.

When my torture finished, all the people in the room clapped. Honest to God, they actually stood up and clapped me, as if I had won a fucking award. 'The Most Useless and Pathetic Consultant in the World', bar none. That's how bad it was.

I wanted to quit right there on the spot. Go back to work for the steering wheel company with the mental MD and the insane, baseball-wielding team leaders. I shuffled to the toilet to compose myself. I splashed water onto my face. I stared at myself in the mirror. I know I fucked up but I didn't deserve to be treated that badly.

The intense debrief at the end of the day couldn't have been more painful if I had pulled my own fingernails out with a rusty pliers. I sat in the car head bowed listening to The Master offering me advice like the bald-headed guy off the *Kung Fu* TV series. Problem was, I wasn't a grasshopper; I was more like a slug; a slug with severe zits crawling slowly over a table of salt. I squirmed with embarrassment in the passenger seat.

By the time I got home I felt a hundred times worse. I didn't speak to anyone. I knew I shouldn't have taken it out on my family, but I just needed some healing time to myself. I sat alone in my small, bedroom office in the dark – upset, angry and emotionally red raw.

Not for the first time I questioned myself. Did I have the balls for the job or was I just fooling myself? I decided to give it another go but made a secret pact that I would never volunteer to work with The Master again. Later that night, when everyone went to bed, I found my daughter's spelling book from school and started to test myself on it.

Like I said, with The Master, it was never personal. At our Christmas piss-up later that year, he took me outside the restaurant to tell me he was sorry about those two days. With tears filling up in *his* eyes he said he really liked me and thought I would be a real asset to the business. Then he started crying. Honest, this mental-headed man, who filled grown men with fear, stood there, tears rolling down his cheeks. (He was pissed at the time, mind.) I started filling up also. I hugged him.

'Right,' he said, wiping his eyes dry, 'send Tom out next.'

And I knew exactly what he was going to talk to Tom about.

One afternoon, a few weeks after my very own Mincer experience, Tom got squeezed to a human pulp in front of me. He was running a morning sales pitch presentation to around forty business men and women in the WDA (Welsh Development Agency) offices in Pontypridd. The aim of the pitch was to get companies signed up to a programme we were running with funded support from the WDA.

I sat off to one side in the front row, my notepad at the ready. Next to me, like a caged tiger, The Master glared and snarled at Tom's every movement. Tom himself was an intimidating man. Touching six feet tall and about the same size wide, in a past life he had been employed by many major companies to take on the unions head-to-head.

He was no mug. But on stage that day, he appeared a bag of nerves. He kept glancing across in our direction. Meanwhile The Master's face grew redder and redder with every perceived mistake Tom made. To the audience, and me, the presentation appeared seamless. To The Master it was blasphemy and someone needed to be crucified. I thanked God it wasn't me standing up there.

With hands shaking Tom placed another slide on the overhead projector.

'It's the wrong fucking slide,' The Master hissed, 'He's fucking this up... he's fucking this... arrrggghhhhhh... fucking hell.' The Master growled loudly. He leapt to his feet and stormed the stage.

He wasn't a big man, maybe five feet five. He marched to where Tom stood, still explaining to the audience about the principles of Lean and how it would benefit their company and the economy of Wales. The Master positioned himself directly in front of Tom. He faced outwards towards the audience.

'Right,' The Master bellowed, 'let me tell you what he should be saying.' He spoke directly over the bigger man. Seconds later, Tom stopped talking altogether; The Master took over the session.

I sat, mouth open, dying to laugh but also feeling so sorry for my new colleague. Some of the audience couldn't help themselves. Many sat doubled over. One guy behind me burst out laughing. He left the room in uncontrollable fits of laughter.

Tom stood behind The Master, sweat pouring from his brow.

It was so excruciating to watch. I felt his pain. God knows what went on in Tom's mind. Slowly, he shuffled sideways off the stage like an embarrassed crab that had farted in a lift full of other shellfish.

After it was over, sheepishly, Tom packed the equipment away.

'You OK?' I asked.

He rolled his eyes.

'The Mincer,' I added.

'Yeah... The Mincer.'

I helped him put the equipment in his car. We went to the pub and had a few beers.

The Master's fearful reputation followed him wherever he went. Yet, strangely enough, unlike some of the other partners, nearly all the consultants in the business liked him. I liked him, a lot. On saying that, no one wanted to work with the evil fucker! I would rather have chewed my right foot off than go through the two days of hell I had been through with him.

The tales about him became legendary and were whispered among us consultants after a few beers. Of how he threatened to suspend one consultant for being too slow while playing one of the simulation exercises. And then wanting to sack the same consultant after he turned a flip chart page over at the wrong time. Apparently, he sacked one guy who accidently dozed off during a lecture (one of his lectures). In front of a packed room, he yelled at the consultant to get his stuff and get out.

But the funniest incident I witnessed first-hand was to do with a phone line and a dull-looking idiot.

For a business at the cutting-edge of industry, we definitely weren't at the forefront as far as technology was concerned when I joined the business. In our main office there was only one phone connection which was also used to get onto the Internet. This was way before Wi-Fi and wireless connections and all that jazz. It meant if someone needed to check their emails they would simply pull the phone plug connections out of the phone and place it into the computer socket. Very Dark Age considering how bright technology is today.

Anyway, one afternoon I sat in the office with The Master helping him to write a proposal worth about a hundred grand for the business. While he wrote it I sat there agreeing with whatever he said and making him coffee. He was extremely focused and not in the best of moods.

After drafting a rough outline of the proposal, The Master wanted to check with the main guy from the WDA that we were on the right track before continuing. He phoned him on the office phone. In the meantime, I started making another serving of The Master's strong coffee.

Minutes later, Chris, the office IT apprentice, sauntered in. Now Chris was a nice boy really, but very green behind the ears. He'd never had a proper job and had no real workplace experience. That wasn't his fault. He was young and straight out of college. But his main problem was that at times he tried to be a lot cleverer than he actually was, which just got on people's tits.

'Crawling to the boss again, are you?' he said sarcastically to me as he sat down at the next desk.

The Master remained too engrossed in his telephone conversation to notice him. Chris opened his computer up and reached across towards the phone plug. I tried to warn him (honest) but I couldn't get the words out quickly enough. I watched in delight as he pulled the plug out of the wall.

The phone line went dead.

It took The Master several seconds before he realised something was wrong. He pressed the keys and shouted hello several times into the receiver. With a confused expression on his serious face he slowly turned around. Chris stood there, caught red-handed holding both connection leads.

'Arrrrggggghhhh,' The Master dived at the fresh-faced boy, arms outstretched. Luckily for Chris, The Master tripped over his computer bag and landed face down on the floor. Chris raced out of the room before The Master got back to his feet. He sprinted out after him, chasing him down the stairs, screaming. In stitches, I ran to the window to watch. Chris got in his car and locked the doors only a millisecond before the bright, red-faced Master reached him. He banged on the window with his fists. Steam escaped from his ears. His eyeballs bulged out of their sockets.

I laughed so much tears rolled down my face. I really wanted Chris to drive away with The Master clutching to the bonnet of the car. It didn't happen. Chris stayed in the car crying until The Master cooled down.

To be fair to Chris, The Master took most of his frustrations out on the lad. Sometimes he deserved it. Other times, thank fuck for the rest of us, he just happened to be in the wrong place at the wrong time.

Watching them was like watching Laurel and Hardy trying to move a grand piano upstairs. I once sat in the back of The Master's car and listened to him ball out the apprentice non-stop from north Wales all the way back to our office in south Wales because he told him to turn left when it should have been right. It was painful to sit through. So painful in fact I prayed for our car to crash over the edge of the mountain and burst into a big ball of flames, even with me in it!

Another occasion, Chris bounded into the office, talking on his mobile and eating a BLT sandwich at the same time. Not looking where he was going, he tripped head-over-tit over the rubbish bin. He landed on his back in the middle of the office. Tom and I sat there pissing ourselves laughing. Not The Master though. He didn't see the funny side. Oh no. From nowhere he materialised over the poor boy. I thought he was going to kick him at first but then he did something worse.

'And which one of the Seven Wastes did you just display there, you useless twat?' he said. I'm sure had he been wearing a bowler hat like Hardy's he would have hit the boy around the head with it.

I glanced at Tom. He made a 'he's gone bonkers' sign using his fingers to his head.

Chris tried to get up.

'No,' the master snapped, 'which of the Seven Wastes did you display?'

'The "He Fell Over A Wastebin Waste,"' I jokingly said.

The Master shot a measured glare at me. I hurriedly carried on with my work. He wouldn't let Chris up off the floor until he had told him what he had done wrong. The Master then wrote the word 'Jerk' on Chris's forehead in marker pen.

The poor boy sat all day like that. I wanted to spit on a hankie like my mother would have done and wipe it off. But I didn't fancy having the words 'Jerk Two' written on my head. I left well alone.

6

Climbing into the Ring
in Tom's Speedos

EVEN CONSIDERING THE Master's Spanish Inquisition style
of management I still felt positive about joining the business.
After a short while it was time for me to get out into the real
world and show what I could do. Tom and Joe, the Welsh pair
of rejects, took me under their devious wings.

For the next year, or so, I spent most of my working life stuck
in cars, sitting in hotel rooms, talking to clients, or relaxing in
the pub with my new partners in crime. Week in, week out, we
drove from one end of Wales to the other trying to blag work
out of companies while trying to keep ourselves alive.

When I worked with Tom, he always drove, no matter what.
I'm not saying he was mild-mannered when he wasn't in a car,
because he wasn't. But placed behind the wheel of his Ford
Mondeo, he turned into a Raging Psychopath with a capital
Raging P.

I never heard so much swearing and so many c-words escape
out of someone's mouth in my life. And I had played rugby in
one of the maddest, swear-filled rugby clubs in the world.

Yet Tom did it with such conviction. In his mind, everyone
else on the road was out to fuck up his journey. He wasn't
having any of it. Once, I listened to him screech out thirteen
'fucks', eight 'you cunts', and enough 'fucking wankers' to fill
a double-decker bus, and we'd only travelled two miles. I used
to tally up his swear words on a piece of paper and reveal all
at the end of the journey. His record took place during a three-
hour trip to west Wales. Not only did he turn the air in the
car blue from start to finish, he made an old woman driving a
Mini cry, and even wound down his window to tell a spaced-
out sheep to fuck off.

Putting his driving insanity to one side, the big man would run through bricks walls for the business. Being a consultant didn't come naturally to him. He had to work at it. He'd been used to directing people all of his life, not being in a role where he was expected to persuade individuals to change. But he wore his heart on his sleeve and I learnt some valuable lessons when we worked together.

At our very first customer visit in a far-off corner of west Wales, he showed me the delicate art of standing up to a bully. The company in St Davids made electronic widgets for kettles and washing machines and such like. A purpose-built unit located well off the beaten track.

The team working with us consisted mainly of shop floor ladies from the production lines. After some basic Lean training, Tom let the women loose to go out and gather some data on various aspects of the business. To be fair, when they understood why we were there, they couldn't wait to get started. Not backwards in coming forward, they highlighted, quite strongly, the amount of money wasted in certain areas.

'We are working too much unnecessary overtime,' said one of the women, 'and for every ten items we make, at least four of them need to be reworked or scrapped.'

She was right. From a quick walk about the main assembly area I saw more bad parts than good. Also many of the staff complained to me how cold it was in the main production area because of the dispatch doors being left open.

With the team on a mission, Tom wanted to prepare the managing director so there would be no real surprises during the feedback presentation at the end of the day.

We both sat in the managing director's nice plush office, located well away from the production areas. From his body language alone I could tell he was something of a first-class brat. Sat bolt upright in his leather chair he seemed aggravated as Tom explained the gist of the findings. He rolled his eyes and scribbled the odd word on the paper in front of him.

I know I shouldn't have butted in while Tom was talking,

but the MD's attitude played on my nerves. We were there to help him not hinder. Yet it felt like we were trying to push a stubborn elephant up a sandbank.

So I piped up, 'And I also think a good gesture would be to get some hot air blowers and put them over the doors in the assembly area. Everyone is complaining how cold it is.'

He looked across at me. His eyes full up with fury. 'Is that what they are saying? They are cold?'

'Yeah,' I nodded, 'I've been down there myself and it is bitter.'

'Well, tell the lazy bastards to either work harder, or wear more clothes to work.' He looked me up and down.

I thought, 'You horrible, selfish twat.' I really wanted to punch him. No, not just punch him, I wanted to reach into my briefcase, pull out a lump hammer and whack the bastard with it. Then roll his crumbled body up in the curtains, drive to the nearest, darkest forest and bury him in the ground with his arse sticking out. That's what he deserved. (Just to clear it up, I didn't carry a lump hammer around in my briefcase in case I bumped into an aggressive managing director and needed to teach him a lesson. But I did have a wicked stapler and an extra-sharp pencil.)

The phone ringing interrupted the awkward silence. He quickly shoo-ed us out of his office. Outside I waited for Tom to give me a dressing down for interfering. He didn't.

'This is going to be bloody interesting,' he muttered. 'Mark my words.'

He wasn't far wrong. During the feedback presentation the MD challenged every point the group brought up. The sad thing was the women had been so positive to start with but now I could see them physically and mentally falling apart. When the amount of rework baskets lying on the floor was mentioned, the MD completely blew his lid. He leapt to his feet. 'Your facts are not correct,' he bellowed, 'this business is doing well.' His rant lasted a full two minutes.

All the team members stared at the floor. To be honest, I

did as well. Tom didn't. He slowly stood up from his seat. I noticed he had his enraged driving face on. 'Everyone out,' Tom motioned to the team. 'Wait outside until I call you back in.'

I went to walk out with them. Tom shook his head at me. I stood way back in the corner. Tom spat his words directly at the MD. 'Do you want to improve, or do you want your head office to ship all of your bloody business off to Europe?' Tom's nostrils flared. 'Do you? Because that's what's going to happen.' Tom puffed out his chest. I couldn't believe this was the same man who turned to jelly weeks before when The Master shamed him during his presentation.

I was afraid to breathe.

'Don't speak to me like that,' the MD replied. 'This is my business. I can say and do as I like.'

That was it. For the next ten minutes the most vicious, hatred-filled, head-to-head screaming match took place that I had ever seen, without actual physical fighting taking place. Both men stood nose-to-nose, spitting insults at each other, their voices at fever pitch. I glanced at the door and saw a woman's head slowly looking over the frosted glass before disappearing again. I was too scared to laugh.

I didn't know what to do. The child in me thought that if I sneaked behind the MD and got down on my knees, Tom could have pushed him backwards onto the floor. Then we could have given him a booting and left.

'OK.' Tom started to pack his things away. He motioned for me to do the same. 'Get somebody else to tell you how bloody good you are. We don't need this. We're off.' Tom didn't look at him.

'Put that in your pipe and smoke it,' I said. Well I would have said it if I had been a proper consultant. But I was in shock, and still a little scared.

On the way out we thanked the team for their efforts. They stared at us like they were a group of cows on their way to the slaughterhouse. I felt sorry for them. On the drive home, Tom didn't swear as much as normal. He still swore more than the average bear suffering from an extreme case of Tourette's, but still quite subdued compared to his usual high standards.

From that moment on Tom became my hero. How he dealt with such an awkward situation took guts. Others would have pandered to the MD. Tom was made of stronger stuff. Rats and snails and Rottweilers' tails. Tom the Terminator, I christened him.

'Don't ever fucking compromise with these pricks,' he said to me. 'If you believe you are right, stick to your guns.' Tough words which would serve me well in future battles ahead.

For our next assignment, we found ourselves in a printing company in the Swansea Valley. The company not only printed the programmes for Swansea City Football Club, they also produced 'prostitute cards'. The ones found in phone boxes in central London. Some of the things on offer would make The 5-Star Gimp blush. I kept a few, just for research purposes, of course.

On a serious note, the major problem they had was getting customer orders out on time. Unbelievably, when Swansea football had a midweek evening match, the company struggled to get the match programmes off the printing press until 7.35 p.m. Problem was, the game kicked off at 7.30 p.m. Not a very good way of keeping their customer, or the supporters, satisfied.

Our role was to find out what was causing these issues and put an implementation plan in place to make sure all deadlines were achieved. That was the easy bit. The more difficult part was trying to stop putting on weight when we were there. Most businesses normally offered us a few sandwiches and bowls of poor quality crisps at lunchtime. Not these guys. Large meat pies covered the boardroom table. I'm not sure if there was a link to the football club or not.

Never mind 'love is a drug'. The gorgeous, meat-filled pies were pure heroin covered in crusts. One bite and we were both hooked. However hard I tried to resist, I couldn't. On a bad day, I munched on three at a time. Tom wolfed down five at each sitting. That meant I ate fifteen calorie-loaded pies in one week... just for lunch. By the end of our second week, I looked like a fucking pie. My hair was all crusty, and my skin flaky. My insides were a bubbling mixture of minced beef and onion. Not a pretty sight!

It wasn't our expanding waistlines, though, which gave Tom the horrors. During one session, held in a small room at the back of the factory, I noticed Tom acting rather strange. When he talked to the group, his eyes kept darting around the room as if following an invisible fly.

'What's the matter, mate?' I asked during a coffee break.

'Can you hear it?' he asked nervously.

'Hear what?'

'The voices.'

'You've ate too many pies,' I joked.

'No seriously. I keep hearing a man's voice.'

'Fuck off!'

'Honest... he keeps saying something.'

I had known Tom long enough by now to tell he wasn't messing about.

I mentioned it to one of the guys. Deadly serious, he told us the room was supposed to be haunted. A few years back, one of the employees, who was having money problems, stacked some chairs up to the ceiling and hung himself from the rafters in the very same room we were in. The way he told the story, it seemed genuine.

I don't know if I imagined it, but suddenly, the room went very cold.

Later that week, after another pie feast lunch, we headed back to the room. Tom unlocked the door. (We locked it because we left our computers and stuff inside.) When we walked inside, we both stood there, mouths wide open. There, in the middle of the floor, all the chairs were stacked up on top of each other towards the ceiling.

Tom went white and actually made the sign of the cross.

Part of me wanted so much to believe the room had really

been haunted by a chair-stacking, hanging-from-the-rafters ghost with money problems. I've always loved horror movies. Or maybe some evil ex-employee, out to bankrupt the business, had been behind it all. A bit like a plot in a *Scooby-Doo* cartoon. Hopefully, an old disgruntled janitor who had been sacked a few years earlier for putting the wrong ink into the wrong bin or something, was looking for revenge.

'Oh… it's Old Man Jones,' Tom would say as he peeled off his mask.

'I would have got away with it as well if it wasn't for you pesky, pie-eating consultants.'

Without doubt, the guys on the course had been playing a trick on us. They probably had a spare key, or had crawled through the extraction duct to set up the chair scene. But they never let on, even when we were leaving.

'It was a fuckin' ghost, I'm telling you. I could fuckin' hear it.' Tom still argues with me to this day.

Another time we worked in a company that had a large ethnic workforce. I took one look around the room and whispered to Tom, 'I can't man the flip charts.' (Not because I'm racist, just because of my fear of spelling.)

'OK,' he said, 'but the pies are on you later.' He was still trying to wean himself off the hot pastry. He was now down to two meat pies a day with chips and gravy.

I agreed. Tom politely asked the first guy in the room his name.

'Derek,' he replied.

Derek went up on the flip chart along with his length of service and job role.

The next girl in line had a similar type of English name. (No, not Derek, that would have been odd.) After writing her details down, Tom turned to the Indian guy by her side.

'Jaspal Singh Khaliqdad,' the man muttered very fast.

Tom looked at him. 'What can I shorten it to?'

'No, my name is Jaspal Singh Khaliqdad. You write Jaspal Singh Khaliqdad please.'

'I know that, but what do people call you.'

'They call me Jaspal Singh Khaliqdad,' he replied stubbornly, with a blank expression on his face.

I'm not sure if the guy was genuine or just taking the piss, or some radical Muslim looking to start trouble with two Western infidels. Tom had to ask him to spell every letter. The next man's name was even longer. I copied it down. (I had a sneaky suspicion I would use it again.)

'Probjot Kanagnalingam Kumar.'

Tom physically shivered when he heard it. It took him about four minutes to write it out in full.

Everyone else's names were quite similar. I was sure by the time we reached the last bloke, that he just made a name up by using every letter in the alphabet about three times over. His first name alone was longer than that long Welsh train station. I sat there, dying to laugh. Under his breath, Tom called me a worthless no good C. But what could I do? I struggled to spell onion bhaji, chicken madras and half-and-half and a poppadum, never mind Probjot Kanagnalingam fuckin' Kumar.

It turned out to be the best pie, chips and gravy I every bought Tom in my life.

Now Joe was a different character altogether to Tom. He was my age, and came from a similar kind of background. Where Tom was older and wore his heart on his sleeve, Joe hid his heart in a shoebox at the bottom of the garden. He'd been with the business for two years before I joined. Deep down he was more of a salesman than a consultant. He talked a good game, but often got others to walk the talk for him. I didn't mind that. Our business needed all types to make it work.

The great thing with Joe was he often said, or did, completely the wrong thing at the wrong time. A Welsh version of *Mister Bean*. He even looked a little bit like him. If there was a situation where someone was bound to put their foot in it, Joe's two feet would be right in there up to his shin bone.

One afternoon he took me on my first sales visit to a client.

I hated selling. I couldn't sell a bottle of ice cold water on a beach full of people if the temperature was ninety degrees.

We sat in my car on a wet, rainy, Wednesday afternoon near Newport docks. The wind howled across the Bristol Channel.

'Right,' he said, 'this is a big one for us. We need to make a big impression.' I'd never seen him so animated or so serious. It meant a lot to him. 'Are you ready?' He looked me in the eye.

I nodded.

'Don't just nod... are you ready?' He gave it a big fist, shaking cry.

'Yes,' I replied, 'I'm ready.'

'Right... let's get in there and fucking do this.' We both yahooed like two dull American college kids. We actually high-fived each other. How embarrassing! Then he opened the car door and just disappeared. I looked across. He'd somehow caught his one foot in the seat belt strap. He lay flat on his face on the ground in the car park in a muddy puddle.

He leapt up. Mud covered one side of his face. His white shirt was now stinking. He clambered back in the car and ducked down so no one could see. For some reason I ducked down as well. I didn't know if I should laugh or cry. I looked at him for direction. I knew we couldn't stay crunched down for much longer. My legs went dead.

'Do you think anyone saw me?' he asked.

'I don't know.' I stuck my head up and looked about. 'Everything looks quiet.'

He started laughing. I started laughing. I laughed so much I thought I was going to have a heart attack.

'Let's go.'

'Where?'

'Just drive.'

I quietly pulled out of the car park. We drove to the nearest McDonalds for him to clean himself up. Luckily, I had a spare shirt in the back. Fair play, he composed himself enough to do an excellent pitch and he closed the sale.

On another sales visit we rocked up at a company in north Wales. The name of the business was quite unusual. Something like Norris Doppleganger.

We got there bright and early. This time he avoided the car park mud wrestling. The owner showed us to the boardroom. There was the usual small talk about the weather and last night's football match as we set up our equipment.

The owner offered us some coffee. Out of the blue Joe piped up without really thinking, 'Norris Doppleganger... Norris Doppleganger... who the hell thought of calling a business such a terrible name?'

The owner's face changed. 'I did,' he said. 'It was my grandfather's name.'

It was one of those 'shall I get my coat?' moments. We laughed like fools on the way home – not surprisingly, without a sale.

But with Joe, his world was littered with those 'shall I get my coat?' moments. Another company made inflatable dinghies for the SAS out in Iraq. I'm still not sure what the SAS did with inflatable dinghies in Iraq. Maybe they raced them down sand dunes in between getting shot at.

Anyway, the production manager was a short guy with a mop of bright ginger hair. He also had buck teeth. He looked like a ginger Bugs Bunny in a cheap Matalan suit. He had definitely been way at the back of the queue when God handed out good looks. Hopefully, for his sake, he was near the front when he also gave out knobs like racehorses and tongues like anteaters.

After a chat about the main issues facing the business, ginger-top casually said, 'By the way I've got to go out to Iraq next week. I bloody hate going there.'

Yet again, without thinking, Joe chipped in, 'Why's that? Because you're ginger and don't like the sun, is it?'

If Joe had been made out of chocolate, the stare from ginger-nut would have melted him on the spot.

'No,' he snapped back. ''Cos there's a bloody war going on.'

Another sales opportunity lost, but as far as our friendship and bonding were concerned, it was priceless.

However, Joe wasn't the only one to screw up. I put my foot in where it didn't belong many times. After being asked by the owner of a painting and decorating company did I think the two managers running the business were up to the job, I made my point as clear and as honestly as I could. 'No, they are both a pair of muppets.' They even looked a bit like Kermit and Miss Piggy.

At that point the owner slumped down into his chair and broke down into tears. 'Those are my two boys,' he muttered.

'Oh fuck,' I thought.

'Thanks,' he said, 'I needed to know the truth.' He seemed more upset I thought his boys weren't up to the mark of taking over his business after he retired than with my comments. Thank God!

Probably the incident I remember most when working with Joe was the Day of the Jackal, or to be more precise, the Morning of the Whippet. My personal development had been going well and it wouldn't be long before I would be let loose by myself. The company we visited was a small family-owned business in mid-Wales. The sales workshop took place in the owner's office which was slightly bigger than a sardine can.

Joe began setting up his equipment at the front. A look of surprise and then horror spread across his face. 'Oh, what the fuck?' he said. 'Bunko, there's a dog under this desk.'

'Shut up.'

'There is... look.'

He wasn't lying. A whippet lay fast asleep in a dog basket in the recess of the desk. A massive bone lay by its side.

'Hey, maybe that's the leg of the last consultant,' I joked.

The dog belonged to the owner. Apparently, he often brought it into work with him.

'What shall we do?' he asked.

'Don't worry; it won't bother you,' I added. 'It's asleep.'

The other guys turned up on time and took their seats next

to me. The owner sent his apologies. He had been called to an emergency meeting with their main customer. Joe started with the usual consultant spiel. But I could tell something was wrong. Every time he went to press the page forward button on his computer, a scared look appeared on his face. He kept glancing furtively under the table. After about ten minutes he stopped.

'This is no good,' he said. 'Can we get rid of the dog? It's snarling at me.'

Everyone crowded around the creature. It growled louder. One guy tried to tease it out by reaching to pick up the bone. It snapped at him. The man jumped back, crashing into a cabinet. Books fell onto the floor.

The dog wouldn't budge.

'Can you operate the computer?' he asked me.

'No way.'

Half-heartedly, Joe started the presentation again. By now no-one in the room, including me and probably Joe, was listening to a word he said. We all sat watching – watching and waiting for the skinny, black beast from under the desk to pounce and rip his hand off.

During a tense five minutes Joe talked, the dog snarled. Then, not unexpectedly, the dog went for Joe. Maybe it could sense his fear. Or maybe it didn't agree with what Joe had been talking about. God only knows. But it was angry. Joe leapt back, and kicked out at the beast. That only made it madder. The dog barked, teeth showing. One of the guys tried to grab its collar. It snapped at his hand, drawing blood. We cornered it. Joe poked it with a chair. The dog fought back. In the end, we left the creature alone and finished the presentation in the canteen. Again, we never got any follow-on work.

Without making it sound all doom, gloom, out-takes and blunders, we did win lots of work without causing too much chaos. And from a personal aspect, I learnt quite a bit about how to deal with some of the more awkward sides of consultant life.

Not long after, I progressed into running a few workshops with support from either Joe or Tom. Most, I am pleased to say, were incident-free. However one thing I quickly appreciated was to never take anything for granted. I ran one Lean workshop in a company in Barry with Tom, at the back, observing my performance. At the feedback session later he scored me very highly and commented on how well I had done.

'I'm the bee's knees,' I told my wife later that night. 'I'm a natural at this consultant stuff.'

'Pity you aren't a natural at doing some DIY around here,' she moaned. 'I need some pictures put up.'

She wouldn't believe my excuse that I was allergic to DIY in any way, shape, or form.

Two days later I confidently strolled into another company in Blackwood in the Valleys to do a similar type of workshop.

Even though the material was, more or less, exactly the same, the session couldn't have gone more differently if I had done it in the style of an Italian opera singer dressed as a traffic warden. The audience, mainly bored, middle-aged women, slumped in their plastic seats, unenthusiastic from the moment I stepped into the room. I don't think it was just me that pissed them off. They seemed to be pissed off about anything and anybody in the world as a whole!

Unlike the group in Swansea who asked questions and talked about improvements, these ladies had no interest at all. They didn't even talk to each other. They sat quietly from the start, rolling their eyes or filing their nails. The very interactive simulation exercise designed to show the group how Lean can help a business improve was anything but interactive. They didn't understand the concept, and, more disappointingly, didn't want to understand the concept. I was quite passionate about continuous improvement but, however hard I tried, begged and pleaded, they sat stony-faced. Mainly they just kept leaving to go to the toilet. Maybe they all had the runs or more likely, a STD. My performance suffered. I lost them before I ever found them. Tom jumped in now and again but even he couldn't rescue the situation.

Tom's feedback at the end of the day was blunt and to the point. In less than three days I had gone from ecstasy to the gates of depression. I questioned myself again. Maybe I wasn't cut out for this role.

'Don't be downhearted,' he said. 'Sometimes in this job you can take a horse to water, but you can't make the stupid, fucking mares drink.'

At least it made me laugh.

That night I tried to put the pictures up in the front room in my house. I failed at that as well. My wife was not impressed!

Although stressful, one of the most exciting parts of the job was the different types of businesses I worked in. It varied so much. One day I would be at a waste water site, wading through shit, sweet corn, condoms, jam rags and even a few mouldy dead dogs. Next, a factory growing snake venom in the bellies of sheep. (Honestly!) Once I went to see a man who made gravestones. He couldn't have been more suited for the job if he tried. A grey and dour-looking bloke in a grey and dour business. He looked like death warmed up by a few degrees. Any hint of a sense of humour drained from his body at birth. All that was missing was the Grim Reaper as his apprentice. He hated people from Cardiff with a passion. After being in a room with him for ten minutes, it became obvious he hated everyone, except for dead people. I wasn't sure if that included dead people from Cardiff – probably did!

He threw me out when I jokingly asked him if he had any issues with customer complaints.

I put it down to part of my learning curve.

After a few weeks I got all the right ticks in all the right boxes, and got signed off by Tom. Next for me was a journey into the brave, new world all by myself. And, as sod's law would have it, my first proper activity collided with an event no-one in the world would ever forget.

7

Is it a Bird, or is it a Plane?

WHAT HAPPENED ON September 11th 2001 will be forever etched in people's minds. On that day I was on my own running, or trying to run, my first big workshop in an aluminium component company.

A group of fourteen people were squashed into a small, hot room in a south Wales factory. Many of the individuals were customers of the aluminum business and had travelled down from Sheffield for the week-long event. We had already been there for a few days trying to find out any wasted activities taking place in the supply chain.

To be frank, I had been a bag of nerves, or in layman's terms, crapping myself, before, during and after each session. I wanted everything to be just right. I wanted to show The Master and the others that I had what it took to be a success in this arena.

It didn't start well. During the first two days, I noticed a twenty-something-year-old boy kept falling asleep when I was presenting. As soon as I spoke, he nodded off. The others in the class nudged and giggled to each other.

'You cheeky, ignorant, sleepy twat,' I thought. I knew I had to sort it out quickly, or the others could fall asleep in protest.

During a coffee break, I pulled him to one side. 'Am I boring you?'

'What?'

'You keep falling asleep.'

'Oh I'm so sorry,' he apologised, 'it's my mother's fault.'

'Your mother?' my one eyebrow touched the top of my forehead. 'What the hell has your mother got to do with it?'

'She used to strap me in my car seat when I was a baby and place it on top of the switched-on washing machine, until I fell asleep.' (I instantly pictured his mother doing the same thing, but for a different reason!) Because of this, whenever he sat in a room where there was a low, rumbling noise in the background, he automatically nodded off. Our room was over the boiler house with a faint, monotonous buzz from the generator down below.

He seemed genuine enough. I wondered what I could do. I considered phoning Tom and ask him for advice. But that was taking the easy way out. In the end I used my loaf and I turned the problem into an opportunity. (See, I was really starting to become a proper consultant, I even began to talk in buzzwords.) What I did was I simply waited for the next time the boy dropped off, then I zapped the lethargic bastard with an electrical cattle prod. It was so funny – you should have seen him jump! No, I didn't. But, I reckon, that would have cured the idle fucker for good. Instead, I got him up on his feet to man the flip charts wherever possible.

Being a consultant, running one of these sessions was a little bit like being a top rated snooker player. I needed to be thinking a couple of shots ahead of everyone else in the room. So other than the Sleeping Beauty incident, up to the morning of the 11th, even if I say so myself, I was doing all right. Everything seemed to be on track and I was quite proud of my progress.

Rather unusually, the company employed a male secretary. To describe Martin, the twenty-two year old with dyed, highlighted blond hair, a soft quiet voice and an outrageous teapot stance, as very, very feminine would have been the biggest understatement of the year. A colourful concoction of a young Graham Norton with a large slice of Mister Godfrey off *Are You Being Served?* thrown in for good measure.

To his credit, Martin was the most efficient person I had come across. Everything I asked him to do, he not only did on time but he did to the highest quality possible. Coffee breaks really allowed Martin to shine. He made the best homemade cakes anyone had ever tasted. I'm not a gateau fan, but his cheese cakes were to die for. Mister Kipling bake your heart out!

Around two o'clock on the Thursday we stopped for a quick break.

'Oh, by the way,' Martin casually mentioned, while cutting a thickly coated double chocolate creation into large slices, 'a plane's just crashed into the Twin Towers.'

To me, it was a throwaway comment. Without sounding horrible, I had more pressing things to worry about than a small, private plane clipping some building in America. Martin didn't say anything else. He was more concerned about what everyone thought of his new offering.

The workshop started back up about twenty minutes later. Not long after Martin popped into the room to clean away any dirty cups and plates. 'Oh, by the way, a second plane has flown into the other tower now!'

Again, I must admit at the time I couldn't really give a rat's arse. I had a deadline to achieve and the group had just spent more than two hours deciding if changing a machine over to a new product was adding value or not.

Minutes, later, Martin raced back in, arms flailing about, and tears streaming down his face. I thought he'd seen a spider or someone told him his cake sucked. 'The planes... the planes,' he sounded like the midget bloke from the TV show, *Fantasy Island*. 'The planes... the planes.'

'Mart... sit down.' He did what I asked. 'Now, slow down... What's happened?'

His voice reached fever pitch. Both hands located on his hips. 'It's on the news in the boardroom. Four planes have gone down in America.' Everyone in the room stood quiet. 'It's war... it's war... we're under attack,' he shrieked.

'Where have the planes gone down?' someone chipped in.

Theatrically, his hand shook as he held a glass of water. 'Two planes have crashed into the Trade Centre in New York... one in Washington.' He took a gulp of water, 'and the other one has gone down in... in... in Transylvania.'

I know it's terrible but the first image to pop in to my mind was of Peter Cushing, looking very intense, while driving a wooden, stake-shaped aeroplane towards Christopher Lee's Dracula castle.

'Transylvania...? That's not even a proper place,' a girl at the back piped up.

'I think he means Pennsylvania,' I corrected him. 'And Transylvania is a place,' I corrected her.

Everyone stopped what they were doing and rushed out to watch the TV in the boardroom. We all stood about in silence watching the dreadful scenes unfolding across the Pond.

'OK, let's get back,' I clapped my hands loudly.

Martin squealed and nearly fainted.

I could tell by the expressions on the others' faces, they didn't care a fuck about how an aluminium pump casting for a washing machine was made. There was a war going on. I had no choice but to postpone the course until the morning. I hoped The Master wouldn't find out.

It's really funny how life works out. A few years later I heard Martin got sacked from the business for doing something rather nasty. He then got a job at Bristol Airport, for a well-known low-cost aircraft company. Apparently, after he got passed over for a promotion, he started to make hoax calls to the airport telling them there were bombs on the planes. He got caught and imprisoned. A real shame for the poor boy. I'm not sure if the events of that day affected him enough to do something so bizarre. On the plus side, at least the inmates of Strangeways Prison, or wherever he found himself, benefited from his exceedingly good cakes.

Not long after, The Master set me up on a sales visit to a business making the brackets and stuff for displays in shops windows. It was a small company with only about fifteen people working there. I was booked in to see the owner for an afternoon slot.

I really wasn't looking forward to my first one-to-one sales presentation at all. Like I said earlier, I am not a salesman – in fact, I hate everything about them. But selling was par for the course. And I saw this visit as my first test from The Master. I didn't want to fuck it up.

The night before, I ran through my presentation several times in the quiet of my bedroom. I sat there alone shitting myself. What made me feel worse was the amount of slides I was expected to present – 137 slides to be exact. In my opinion, 134 slides too bloody many.

'Stick to the script,' The Master warned me during my induction training. 'No ad-libbing, no straying, and whatever happens, never, ever miss out a slide... *or else.*'

He never said what the 'or else' would be, but I could imagine it had something to do with pliers and toenails. He still scared me half to death.

I felt like a robot as I went through the presentation over and over again. Maybe it would have been better just to programme R2D2 to go in and beam it onto the wall on our behalf. At least it would have saved me from selling my soul for a few days at £450 a day, plus mileage.

That morning, like a well-drilled soldier, I marched off in double quick time. It was before the age of sat nav, so I set off early in case I got lost. I did get lost and ended up driving into a pig farm. A quick U-turn later and I managed to still arrive on time. The secretary showed me into the owner's messy, paper-laden, old-fashioned styled office.

'Mr James will be with you shortly,' she said.

First thing I did was check for whippets or other deadly creatures hiding under the desk. It was pet-free. On saying that, an elephant could have been hiding under the stack of papers, empty cups and old books on his desk and I wouldn't have known. The room looked a complete mess. I counted at least four mouse traps dotted among the rubbish. One actually had a dead, rotten mouse in it.

I couldn't place my computer on the old oak desk without

moving several trees worth of paper. I placed the stuff on the floor next to another forest worth of documents.

If the factory looked anything like his office, the first thing needed would be to clean the place up properly. I made a mental note to emphasis this point during the presentation. I wasn't as dull as I looked!

The owner arrived ten minutes later, holding a coffee mug with the words 'I'm the Boss' printed on it. Just by looking at his dirty, baggy check shirt and oily fingernails, I could tell he was more at home making things than cleaning his office or listening to a wanker like me trying to tell him what I could do for his company.

With my mind focused on hitting my sales quota, I took a deep breath and began. Slides one, two, three and even a bit of four went all right. My voice sounded shaky, but I didn't think he noticed. He sat nodding and rubbing his chin a lot.

I carried on. I'm not sure if someone hit the thermostat or if I was going through the change! I could feel rivers of sweat flowing down the cheeks of my arse. There was no air conditioning, not even a window. I soldiered on, sipping lukewarm water.

By slide ten, which showed a horrendously complicated model of policy deployment, I had lost the will to live. God only knows how he felt. I wished I had a razorblade with me, or that bloody lump hammer.

The more bullshit I spoke, the hotter the room got. I tried to look and sound confident. I didn't feel it was working. Slide twelve proved to be the beginning of the end. His eyes got heavier and heavier, and then mid-sentence, they closed completely.

I waited, holding my breath.

He slumped back in his chair, motionless. He had fallen asleep. Fuck me, perhaps the boy who told me the car seat on the washing machine story had been telling lies. Maybe I had been that boring? Including Washing Machine Boy, I had sent two people fast asleep in subsequent visits. I wondered if I would get a mention in 'The Guinness Book of Useless Consultant Facts': 'Anthony Bunko made his victim... sorry, client... fall fast asleep by slide thirteen, unlucky for some, or maybe just bloody lucky for us both?'

I stopped talking. I didn't know what to do. Should I carry on or wait politely for him to wake up? He looked like the type who probably only slept for about twenty-three minutes a day and then he most likely dreamt of combustion engines.

I coughed.

Nothing.

Hang on, what if he was dead? He hadn't moved. My mind went off on a bizarre tangent. 'Murderer,' I could hear people screaming at me as I pushed a trolley around Tesco.

'It was the presentation... the presentation I'm telling you, not me... I don't bore people to death,' I cried back.

They wouldn't listen. They grabbed tins of baked beans to stone (or can) me with. I pictured Tom and Joe laughing their heads off when my face popped up on the Welsh news.

Thank God, the bloke finally snored. 'Thank fuck, he is only sleeping,' I whispered quite proudly, as if that was acceptable. Well I guess it was better than killing him.

I let him sleep. He looked like he needed it. I studied his features. Bags dragged his eyes down to meet his cheeks. His hair was a shock of white. His ears and nose so big they looked like a cartoonist had drawn them and stuck them on his face.

I got bored and looked about. A large portrait of an elderly, stately man hung on the wall. I assumed it to be a relative, a great-great-granddad maybe who started the business in 1818. I could have been wrong. As far as I knew he could have bought it in a car boot sale. (The photo of the gentleman, not the business.)

I couldn't just sit there thinking of crap. I had to do something. Unbelievably I pushed the button on the

77

computer and moved on to the next slide. Oh no, a slide on culture change! I quickly glanced behind me in case The Master was hiding in the cupboard waiting to pounce. He wasn't. I skipped on a few slides. Well, quite a few actually.

I carried on talking to the sleeping man but in a quieter tone. Part of me wanted him to sleep until the end. 'There are five Lean principles,' I whispered. The evil devil on my shoulder wanted to add in a demonic accent, 'And the fifth principle is, your mother sucks cocks in Pontlottyn.'

Suddenly, the phone rang, loudly. I shrieked. He jumped straight up onto his feet like a boxer on hearing the bell. He glared at me. 'How many more slides are there, mate?'

'Hum... only about ninety... odd.'

He paced about, 'Oh... just give me the paper to sign.'

And that was it. I had sold my first tranche of work by boring the guy half to death. Chuffed to bits, I drove to the office to hand in my first sales success.

'Only five bloody days of work,' The Master looked at the form. 'There was at least twenty days of work in there.' With kettle in hand he stormed out of the office.

Deflated, I trudged back to my car. Once outside, I stood in the car park and screamed loudly before driving home.

As the weeks moved on, I grew more confident in what I was doing and why I was doing it. Although I felt like I was getting better, I wanted to get better faster. To do that, I needed to work with the best.

Out of all the die-hard consultants strutting their stuff, no one strutted it better than The Glass Is Always Half Full partner. Although regarded as a young pup compared to the other partners, I'd been informed he had been born to lead workshops. Apparently, he could do everything. Sell, talk, dance, be funny, be serious, and juggle with five flipchart markers at the same time. Clients loved him. Partners envied him.

Determined to get better, I asked The Glass Is Always Half Full partner if I could shadow him on a few workshops. I was hitting my monthly revenue targets, so a few shadowing days wouldn't go amiss. He agreed.

I bought a tape recorder so I could record him while he was doing his presentations. It wasn't like the old-type recorders I used to tape the Christmas *Top of the Pops* when I was growing up in Dowlais Flats. You know, the one where you held the mike up to the speaker of the telly while telling your drunken father to shut up. This was more hi-tech.

I sat at the side of the room recording every word he said during the workshop. Along with that I scribbled notes on his every movement. Even down to his facial expressions.

Each night I went home and played it back. I made notes. I walked around the bedroom copying his mannerisms, his expressions, even his hand gestures. I stalked – sorry – shadowed him whenever I could. Stupidly I not only wanted to copy him, I think I wanted to be him. A mini-me version of The Glass Is Always Half Full. (The Glass Is Nearly A Quarter Full consultant.) I even considered dying my hair ginger. With hindsight, how dull was I? I could never have gone into my local rugby club with ginger hair!

During one event at a posh hotel to a group of very senior managers, he asked if I would like to lead one or two of the easier exercises. I was chuffed. It was a big step up.

Brimming with self-confidence, The Glass Is Always Half Full partner opened up the session like Status Quo kicking off Live Aid at Wembley. He quickly set the scene while getting the audience in the right frame of mind. His voice boomed around the room with authority, yet without sounding brash or arrogant. Everyone laughed at his jokes. Every single person in the room sat there smiling. He remembered everyone's name within the first five minutes. His rapport with the group was as if he had known them all of his life. I sat in the wings wishing I hadn't agreed to do anything. He amazed me. He knew how to answer a question with a question better than any politician on the block.

Following Tom and Joe was daunting enough when starting

out, but this was a different ball game. I felt like I was about to go out on stage with an out of tune guitar just after the Beatles and Elvis Presley finished their sets.

I tried to keep positive. My arse flapped like a bird's wing.

'I'll be OK... I'll be OK,' I told myself.

But what if I fuck up? What if I call one of them a no-good slimy motherfucker for no reason? Unlikely, but what if I had somehow contracted Consultant Tourette's, and I didn't know? What if I shat myself? Here I go... the shitting myself again thought. I needed to see a doctor or a shrink or at least get a butt plug.

After the next coffee break, it would be my turn to run the simple exercise about buying tins of beans in a supermarket. I'd done the exercise before, but to a much smaller, and less senior group of individuals. Senior managers made me nervous anyway.

I rushed to the toilet for a pee to calm my nerves. I looked at myself in the mirror. I didn't look as nervous as I felt. Then disaster struck. While washing my hands I turned the tap on too fast. Water splashed all over my cream chinos. It looked like I had pissed myself. I wanted to die. I spent five minutes trying unsuccessfully to dry up the stain on the front of my pants. It didn't work. My time was up. I wandered out to the front of the room like a man walking to the gallows.

'Sorry,' my voice shook, 'I didn't pee myself honest... It's water from the toilet.' I thought at least it would get me a sympathy laugh.

Nothing. Not even a chuckle.

'Oh fuck,' I thought, 'where's my bloody coat?'

What little confidence I had drained away along with my colour. I began handing out sheets of paper with the exercise on it. I dropped some of the papers on the floor. I got flustered.

I explained what I wanted them to do, but I could tell by their faces I was talking too fast and too Welsh. But I couldn't slow down. My accent somehow went from mild-sounding Welsh to speeded up eighteenth-century Druid Welsh. Even

I couldn't understand what I was saying, and I was fucking saying it. I lost all comprehension of full stops or commas in my sentences.

I could feel sweat patches soaking my armpits. I lost track of where I was in the exercise and where I should have been at what time. I fell apart. I could sense the disappointment and anger in the room. The Glass Is Always Half Full partner nodded his support from the wings for a while. But in the end he jumped in before I fell straight off the edge of the cliff and broke any credibility I had into tiny pieces. He took over and led the group not only through that one exercise, but for the rest of the day. That's how bad I had been.

I sat swaying in the corner like a mental patient in a nuthouse. I watched my boss save the situation. I wanted to quit. I was just fooling myself. Ladbrokes would have given better odds on me becoming a nun than on me making it as a proper consultant.

I felt a million times worse than the day I'd got squeezed through The Mincer by The Master. At least that hadn't really been my fault. I was set up to fail. But this time I had supposedly been prepared. Yet, like the *Titanic*, I sank badly at the first sighting of an iceberg.

My nightmare was far from over. What made it worse was the group of managers had been asked to score the consultants on their performance of the day. We sat in the car analysing the scores. Of course, The Glass Is Always Half Full partner scored almost perfect tens. One woman actually gave him a twelve. He was good but not that bloody good. She probably fancied him. I started to hate him with a passion. The smooth-talking, ginger-haired freak!

I had been lucky to register on the manager's scorecards. One person simply scribbled across the feedback sheet: 'If Anthony had been a wounded horse, I would have shot him.'

It makes me laugh now but, at the time, I wish he had fucking shot me, right between the eyes.

I think the problem was, I wasn't being myself. I was trying to be him, Mister Bloody Perfect partner. But, however hard I tried, I was never going to be a 'glass is always half full' type of person. I was more of the 'mug has fallen off the kitchen unit and is smashed and a rat is drinking all the milk off the floor' kind of bloke.

I learnt my biggest lesson that day. Trying to be somebody I wasn't, wasn't going to work. I needed to find my own voice, my own style and identity. Of course, it's good to observe and get tips off others, but don't copy them.

I did some soul-searching. We had recently introduced a psychometric test in the business designed to tell us if a possible new recruit would be suited to become a consultant. I asked the Human Resources person could I do one just to see what I needed to do to improve. Before giving me my results back, she said (honestly!), 'Do you own a motel? And is your mother still alive?'

'No, I don't. And yes, she is.'

'Are you sure?' she asked again before handing me the report on my profile.

My profile results definitely weren't a good match for the role I was in. The characteristics of a good consultant are someone who is an outgoing, confident extrovert. A person who can think on their feet and not bore people to death when they open their mouth. Basically, I came out as a dark and disturbed introvert, with no benefits whatsoever. It more or less said I was suited to working in libraries or starring in horror films.

OK, I exaggerate a little. But I'm convinced if I had been given the test at my initial interview, I wouldn't have got the job.

With that in mind, I knew if I was going to succeed in this business I needed a plan so that I could work to my strengths and hide my weaknesses under the fucking carpet!

8

Attack from the Annoying Midget

As GOLFER GARY Player once said, 'The harder I practise, the luckier I get.' That was also true for me. I worked hard and practised, practised and practised. I grew more confident and, I guess, luckier!

After a year or so I had outgrown the goldfish bowl of Wales. Driving to north Wales on narrow B roads behind tractors and swerving to miss spaced out sheep high on magic mushrooms had now got on my tits. I needed a new challenge. The pleasing thing was, the partners thought so too. They wanted me to move up and to play with the big boys, in the big league.

Therefore, I left Tom and Joe and the rest of the Welsh gang and became a fully-fledged member of the Industry Team. It really was the big time! Working with large, blue-chip clients located all over the world. To land a big contract with some of these guys was worth hundreds of thousands of pounds a year. To celebrate, I invested in some new trousers, a few new shirts and a four-wheel drive Land Rover.

My first piece of corporate work happened to be with a large, European-based Italian company supplying a major fast food business with all their cups and cartons. The company had several sites all over Europe. My assignment was to work in their godfather plant near Naples, and a site in Portugal, but first off I was asked to go and observe the day-to-day activities at their Welsh site.

I'd never worked with Italians before. I'd been in school

with a couple of them, but they kept themselves to themselves and always seemed to be working in their father's cafés.

'Coffee,' my father said to me. 'Italians love lots and lots of coffee, and football and shooting people.'

I think he acquired this knowledge by watching the World Cup and gangster movies.

The football and the shooting I could cope with, but I've never been a big coffee lover. I'm strictly a one cup of coffee a day man. And if the truth be known, I'd rather instant than fresh, ground coffee anyway. I know in some Latin quarters that's a crime punishable by death, but I'm a Merthyr boy through and through.

'Send the Valley Philistine to the electric chair your honour!' someone shouted out in an Italian accent.

But I can't help it. And since I'm spilling the beans here, another dirty little secret of mine is I'd rather eat Smash instant potato than real mashed potato. (That was my mother's fault. She couldn't cook potatoes or much else... sorry, Mam xx.)

Anyway, my father wasn't far wrong. Everywhere in the offices there were free, self-service coffee machines dotted about. Each one usually surrounded by gangs of Italian managers necking back double espressos like they were eating Smarties, while talking in Italian about football and shooting people, I assumed! Then they would all go sprinting off to emergency meetings more wired up than Baz from the Happy Mondays on a freaky Saturday night at the Hacienda.

Every meeting was an emergency meeting. I even went to a few emergency, emergency meetings. Even the ones that started out as non-emergency meetings suddenly became full-on, state of emergency, emergency meetings as soon as an Italian manager joined it halfway through, eyes bulging and smelling of coffee.

My first assignment in the factory was to design and put in place guidelines to control these meetings. A code of conduct was drawn up. No arriving late or leaving meetings early for coffee fixes were high up on the list. Also, no violent hand waving, aggressive shouting, or rolling about on the ground complaining like one of their football stars.

The MD enforced it immediately. The coffee-guzzling Italians weren't happy. The way they glared at me as I walked past them I thought I'd wake up the next morning with a horse's head or a jar of extra strong Nescafé blend in my bed.

After that small success, the MD asked me to link up with a Japanese guru who had been working in their factory to improve the efficiency of their machinery. He was an expert in TPM (Total Preventive Maintenance), a technique made famous by the Japanese after the war when they travelled to the West and pinched our ideas and refined them. The Japanese are the best consultants when it comes to pinching ideas, adapting them and giving them their own name. Fair play to them!

I had some reservations about working with another consultancy, to be honest. Until I started at BS Consulting, I never realised how much rivalry went on between consultancy companies. A lot like football fans. They hated each other.

Without exaggerating, if a consultant was found with his throat slit in a prison cell, and that cell was full of real, dark, scary characters, the likes of Jack the Ripper, Sweeney Todd, John Wayne Gacy, Fred and Rose West and a consultant from a rival firm, I know who I would have my money on as to who dunnit. Enough said!

I once saw The Prof and a rival Prof (who also looked like he was the other last boy to get picked in the schoolyard football match) eyeballing each other in the foyer of a hotel in Cardiff Bay. They scowled at each other like two heavyweight fighters in a boxing ring. Full-on, silent stares as both men moseyed past each other, clutching copies of their latest publication in their grubby fingers. Part of me wanted to shout out 'fight' and see both, well-respected consultancy gangs scrapping it out in the hotel car park. *West Side Story* style!

For this reason, I didn't fancy working with a rival. And

the way they talked about this guy (let's just call him Mister Miyagj), I expected him to walk on water and shit lightning bolts.

The MD called me to his office. 'I would like you to work with him to take the factory to the next level,' he said.

I couldn't get out of it. So I decided to go along for the ride. And who knows? Perhaps it would give me the opportunity to see what I could learn, aka pinch, off the TPM guru from the Far East.

*

My first meeting with the famous Mister Miyagj took place in the boardroom a week later. He was your typical-looking Japanese businessman. Studious features which rarely cracked a smile. I shook his hand with a firm but friendly handshake. I smiled on purpose.

Suddenly, a 'small' guy with a beard pushed up to me. 'Hello, I'm Bernard. I'm the guru's interpreter.'

I looked down at him quite shocked. I didn't expect Mister Miyagj not to be able to speak, or understand, English (well, unless he wanted to!). Not only didn't he speak a word of Queen's English except for 'hello' and something that sounded like 'corn beef stew', but when he spoke he had a strong lisp.

The whole episode had disaster written all over it. Me, a Japanese guru with a lisp and a midget interpreter who, I was sure, I had seen getting thrown across a bar in a pub in my hometown. How very entertaining.

To prove my point, it took over twenty minutes just to get through the introductions. Mister Miyagj looked down at the midget while I looked at Mister Miyagj. Mister Miyagj spoke with a lisp in Japanese to the midget. I looked down at the midget. The midget explained to me what Mister Miyagj with the lisp had said. The Italian managers looked at me, then Mister Miyagj, but not at the midget. I wasn't sure if they feared midgets or just didn't respect them. I looked at Mister Miyagj and replied. He looked at the midget, who told him what I had said. What's more, when the midget translated what the Japanese guy had said, he did it with a lisp. When the midget told Mister Miyagj what I had said, he didn't have a lisp. I wanted to say to him, why the fuck was he translating half the conversation with a lisp? But I didn't. It was only our first meeting. I would keep that old chestnut until another time.

In the end I got a stiff neck from all the looking up and down. At one point I wanted to pick the midget up and plonk him on a chair, so we would all be at the same height. But I didn't have the nerve and, like I said, it was our first get-together.

The introduction fiasco went on for so long I started talking with a bloody lisp. It all ended when Mister Miyagj shouted something about corn beef stew and rushed out of the room waving his arms like a mad man. I thought he had a case of Deli Belly from the sausage rolls.

'We must follow him,' the interpreter said.

'Not if he's going for a shit,' I said.

The interpreter glared at me with his little screwed-up face.

We rushed down the stairs on the trail of the mad Japanese Maharishi. We found him wandering on the shop floor, proudly pointing at a line of machines.

'We work on these machines together,' he said to me in not too bad English.

I looked at the midget. He went to interpret.

'Don't you dare,' I warned him.

That night I went out for a meal with the management team, the guru and the midget. It sounded like a title for a new Disney film. Halfway through the meal, Mister Miyagj closed his eyes. I nudged the purchasing director next to me. 'Look, he's asleep.'

'He's not,' he whispered. 'He's awake. He knows everything that's going on.'

'Bollocks,' I thought, 'this guy is a bigger con man than Del Boy Trotter.' I looked over to where the interpreter sat on a chair on a large cushion. If he had been pretending 'not to sleep' as well, I would have chucked a glass of water over him.

I wondered what would have happened if Mister Miyagj tried pulling a stunt like 'I'm not sleeping, I'm just checking my eyelids for holes' trick if he had come out with us on a BS Consultant team building night. I guarantee he would have woken up minus one eyebrow and the word 'Jerk' written on his head in lipstick, in Japanese, spelt with a lisp!

'He's sleeping,' I said to the purchasing guy again.

The man shook his head. 'No... he's listening.'

I so much wanted him to start snoring at that moment or fall back off the chair and land with his feet up in the air, dying, fly-style. I crossed my fingers in hope.

Thirty minutes later the guru woke up, or stopped 'listening'! He muttered something about corn beef stew, wiped the sleep from his eyes and went home to sleep some more. Struggling to keep up, the little interpreter raced after him.

For all his weird ways, Mister Miyagj was very good at what he did. The machines on the shop floor purred like pussy cats and the company definitely benefited from the old, sleeping owl's wisdom. We worked quite well together and I nicked lots of stuff off him. Result!!

A few weeks later I flew out to Naples to the god-factory. The place which held all the power and the purse strings. I arrived very late at the hotel after being delayed in Milan. The hotel was positioned amid a huge industrial estate. As the taxi drove through the dark streets, I couldn't help but notice the number of prostitutes standing on the street corners. I must have seen around fifty in a two-mile stretch.

Early the next morning, a taxi took me to the gatehouse. It looked more like a prison than a factory. In fact I had more chance of getting into Swansea nick. The guard, armed with a gun and a suspicious frown, demanded my passport.

'I don't carry it around with me,' I tried to explain.

He shrugged his shoulders and carried on doing something

else. I stood there like a lemon. There was a bit of a stand-off between us, which I didn't have a hope in hell of winning. In the end I got a taxi back to my hotel to get it.

When I eventually got inside, I was greeted by a double-strength espresso coffee handed to me by a frumpy-looking Italian lady. She showed me to the boardroom and told me someone would be along soon.

I liked the look of the room, very stylish. Cool, red leather chairs, modern art paintings on the walls and weird sculptures in every corner. I've always loved things like that. One piece of sculpture, made out of old electrical circuit boards and modelled on the New York skyline, caught my eye.

Without thinking, I took a photo of it and a few of the other pieces. The Italian woman entered as I was taking my last snap. She went bonkers. She started screaming and yelling in Italian. Where was that fucking little interpreter when I really needed him? I thought. With her face screwed up into a tight ball, she marched out.

I didn't know if her outburst had something to do with the coffee stressing her out, or if she had a bad case of Italian PMT. Apparently the worst kind of PMT known to mankind, or womankind!

Minutes later, she marched back in, along with two, big, security guards with hand pistols.

'Camera?' she held out her hand.

'What?'

'No photos... give me your camera.'

'No,' I laughed, 'you don't understand... I was only taking photos of the art.' I pointed at the statue. 'Not the factory... I like art... I like paintings,' I waffled, 'I had a B in art O-level.'

They stared at me. Another Italian stand-off which again I had no chance of winning occurred. One of the security guards ambled towards me, his hand on his holster. Shaking, I handed my camera over. The woman grabbed it and deleted everything I had on there. Even my holiday snaps. Then I thought I was going to be the one who got whacked with a lump hammer, thrown into the boot of a car and driven off into the darkest forest to be buried with my arse sticking out of the ground.

That moment set the tone for a very unmemorable week. Everyone I met during the day gave me the cold shoulder. No one talked to me. It pissed me off. I began to hate my job. I was there to help but I felt like Martin Luther King speaking at a KKK rally.

After work, I was too scared to leave my hotel. Like I said, the dark streets were lined with prostitutes, pimps and creepy-looking punters. The three Ps at a prostitute convention. I watched from my bedroom window. Not in a pervy way. I found it fascinating, but also depressing. Cars pulled up constantly. Young girls clambered in, sometimes two at a time. The cars disappeared into the night. Twenty minutes later, the girls would be dropped back off to go through the same ordeal over and over again. I even saw one old guy getting gobbled off in a doorway. It wasn't a pretty sight. He yelled out like a scorched cat.

I felt sick and so hypocritical. There was I, moaning about having to deal with awkward people, while these girls sold their bodies for what? Who knows?

The more I sat staring, the more I realised our professions weren't so dissimilar. We both worked very long and odd hours. We both got paid for keeping clients happy. I got paid more than them, I guess. In the prostitute world they had to keep their pimps happy. In my world, the partners were my pimps. Fucking hell, I bet The 5-Star Gimp would really like that!

And just like hookers, I spent most of my time in hotel rooms (which my clients paid for) lying on my back, staring up at the ceiling and wondering what the fuck was going on. And finally, we both charged by the hour and were willing to do odd things if the price was right. The two oldest professions in the world.

By the time of my last day of dealing with the coffee-mad, secretive Mafia managers, I couldn't wait to get back home. Relieved, I queued up in Naples airport. I just wanted to get through customs and neck a large glass or two of red wine and forget about it all. At the check-in desk I searched about for my passport. Oh, no! I remembered I'd left it in the security gatehouse. I explained in pigeon English to the blank-faced woman waiting to book me in. She shrugged and moved me to one side.

On the verge of freaking out, I quickly phoned my contact at the factory which was forty miles away. He said he would send it in a taxi. I waited, the clock ticking away. If I missed the flight the next one would be the same time the following day. I paced back and forth outside the terminal. I imagined the passport sitting alone in the back seat with a small seat belt across its front page.

Eventually, the taxi pulled up. The guy handed me my passport.

'Seventy Euros,' he demanded.

I only had forty on me.

I handed it to him, shrugged my shoulders and rushed off before he could argue. I raced through the boarding gate to get back home. Maybe driving to north Wales with Tom wasn't so bad after all.

But, I didn't have time for my feet to touch the ground before I was off again. Next stop on my European tour, the land of the dancing queen.

I thought playing rugby, out on the wing, on top of a mountain in Dowlais, was the coldest place in the world. But nothing prepared me for the week I spent in Sweden in March. I hate the cold. I'm allergic to it. Just like DIY.

'Wrap up warm,' one of the other consultants advised me.

I packed an extra jumper, some T-shirts, extra socks, and thick gloves. If I had known then what I know now, I would have added a Snorkel parka like I had in school with the fake fur around the hood. In fact I would have taken Snorkel everything – Snorkel shirts, Snorkel jumpers, even Snorkel pants and socks and a few hot water bottles.

*

My host picked me up from the airport. He looked exactly like one of the guys out of Abba. The one with the beard who played the organ, Benny I think his name was. On saying that, everyone I saw looked like him. Either I was snow blind, or Benny, the frisky songwriter, had been dipping his super trouper into lots of the Mamma Mias.

Sadly, none of the women I saw looked anything like the sexy blonde out of the same supergroup. Most of them looked more like Russian shot-putters. The ironic thing was, when I went to Russia (later chapter) most of the women did look like the sexy blonde girl out of Abba (even the red-haired ones). They even wore clothes from the Seventies.

When I arrived in Sweden it was snowing. When I left five days later it was still snowing. The whole place was bastard freezing! I couldn't stop shivering as Benny's love child drove me to the town. When we pulled into the factory car park, he connected a portable heater up to the car battery. He said, otherwise, by the time we finished work the engine would have frozen up.

Now that's what I call cold.

The company I was working in was a medium-to-large-sized steel mill, which produced steel for the country's car industry. Volvo, I assumed. The favourite car of the carpet-selling gypsies of the UK.

After a steaming mug of coffee, I dressed up like an Eskimo and toured the facility. Everywhere I went, men, women and even the factory polar bear chewed slugs of tobacco. Disgustingly, they all seemed happy to gob lumps of black liquid all over the floor. No one smiled. In fact they showed very little expression at all. All I saw them do was chew tobacco, stamp their feet to try to keep warm and eat pickled herring.

When in Rome, I thought, and I had a go. Eating pickled herring not chewing tobacco. The fish wasn't as bad as it looked or sounded.

After a dull, cold and pickled herring, foot-stamping-packed day, I couldn't wait to get to my hotel. I longed for a nice, long, bubble-filled hot bath and some nice, warm grub. It was already pitch black when I arrived at the old, country mansion set in its own grounds.

An elderly, creepy woman, with piercing blue eyes checked me in.

'Busy tonight?' I enquired, trying to make polite conversation.

'No,' she grunted, 'you are the only one booked in here... all week.' I know it was probably my imagination but I was certain when she smiled, fangs protruded from the corner of her mouth. Maybe it was two slabs of tobacco, I wasn't sure.

A shiver raced down my spine and stuck its head up my ring piece.

Fuck me, I was booked into Bates Motel, all alone, all week, with the Swedish version of Anthony Perkins in a mega-thermal fitted dress. When she showed me to my room, I'm positive there was no reflection of her in the hallway mirror.

Predictably, my room didn't have a bath, only a shower! A shower with an old-style shower curtain. I bet she (or maybe it was a he) took the bath out on purpose, so she, or he, could sneak up on me holding a kitchen knife while I washed my hair.

I wondered if I could get away without showering for the entire week. I sniffed my armpits. No, I needed a wash badly. Leaving the shower curtains open, I jumped in and out of the water as if I was the wicked Witch of the West.

To add to the creepiness, there was no Internet and I couldn't get a connection to my mobile. I was convinced she had cut my mobile phone line. How the hell she had done that I didn't know, but by then my mind had tipped over the edge into horrorville.

I went down for dinner in the restaurant. It was me, and a ticking clock. Everything on the menu, of course, had a pickled herring twist to it. Mashed, fried, boiled, and, of course, pickled. I went for pickled herring soup with homemade pickled herring bread, followed by pickled herring steak and pickled herring potatoes and pickled herring salad, with plenty of salt and herring.

Later, I lay in bed like the little boy in the film *Sixth Sense* with my cold breath swirling out from my mouth. I wasn't sure if it was because my heater-less room was so cold or the place was actually haunted.

'I can see people.'

Only problem was, I couldn't see any bloody people at all. There was just me, myself and I, along with the creepy, old woman who by then I was convinced was not only psycho, but also part werewolf, vampire, ghost, demon and the clown from the movie *It*.

To make matters worse, my room creaked and groaned. Weird noises rose out of every nook and cranny. I remembered Tom's hanging ghost from the printing company. I dared not look under my bed. My parents should shoulder some of the blame for letting me watch scary movies when I was a tot.

Just when I was thinking how stupid I was, someone knocked on my door. I screamed and actually put my head under the blankets. I was nearly forty years of age and I thought if I hid under the blankets a ghost or psycho killer couldn't find me. Never mind my parents, I now blamed all those episodes of *Scooby-Doo*.

Someone, or something, knocked again. My imagination was now in full-on Alfred Hitchcock mode.

In my mind, the twins from *The Shining* hovered outside. Or perhaps, the old woman had gone cabin crazy like the character Jack Nicholson played. 'All work and no play... make the creepy woman a right raving, fucking lunatic.' I pictured her smashing through the door with an axe held in her webbed fingers. 'It's OLGA,' she yelled, while poking her head through the smashed door slats.

'Hello,' I finally whispered.

'Tea?' a woman's voice answered back.

'What?'

'Tea?... for you?'

I opened up the door slowly. The old woman stood there holding a tray with a pot of tea and a few biscuits on it. I took it off her, smiled and slammed and double locked the door. She floated away.

That was nice of her, fair play. But then I thought, 'What if she's drugged it? What if she's ground some sleeping tablets up in there and I'll wake up tied to the bed like the writer in *Misery*?' I winced as I thought of her crushing my ankles with a lump hammer, then making me write an entire book about pickled herring.

But I was too cold not to drink it. I survived.

All week she kept knocking my door at odd times and handing me a tray of tea. I came to the conclusion she wasn't a murderer or a monster at all, but the Swedish version of Mrs Doyle off *Father Ted*.

'Go on... go on... have a cup of tea.'

For the rest of the week, as soon I finished work, I more or less went straight to bed. I didn't eat. I didn't wash. I just sat in my bed watching the cold air from my breath and waiting for my tea and biscuits.

After it was over, Sweden was another place ticked off my list.

*

Although travelling to bizarre places took up lots of my time, I still felt there was something a bit more creative out there for me. I had reached the grand old age of forty and, surprisingly, I hadn't yet turned completely into my old man. I was getting greyer and a little heavier but as long as I was moving forward and not stuck, or worse still, moving backwards, I didn't care. I've always hated people who lived out their lives looking backwards instead of forwards.

I never set out to write a book. I think it found me rather than me going out of my way to find it. I remember the day it happened so well. Not long after Sweden I travelled to Iceland.

Not the country, the supermarket chain just outside London. After a successful workshop I was returning home on the M4 on a sunny, Friday afternoon.

I called my wife and asked if she fancied taking the family out for some grub to celebrate me coming home before 7 p.m. on a Friday for the first time in ages.

I was in a great mood. Then I hit it. An eight-mile traffic jam stretching all the way back from the English side of the Severn Bridge. The woman on the radio traffic report said there had been a major accident and it wouldn't be cleared for several hours.

I was trapped. I couldn't get off. I phoned the family back to tell them not to bother getting togged up. It would be a takeaway, or Pot Noodles, again tonight!

'Bollocks!' Best laid plans and all that.

I wanted to scream. I sat there frustrated and angry. Anger turned to boredom. I'd had an idea for a story in my head for a while. I had just come back from a long weekend rugby tour with my mates to Portugal. Before I'd gone I watched a fascinating programme on Sky about a gang of horny Bonobo monkeys having sex all day, every day. The male monkeys shagged the female monkeys constantly. When not shagging them, they masturbated and worse still had sex with young monkeys. It was like a hairy tribe of Russell Brands; my Uncle Trevor, who got caught masturbating in Woolworths, and Gary Glitter, all rolled up into one.

During a drunken afternoon sat in a plastic, Paddy pub in Portugal overlooking the sea, I told my mate Gary Morgan about the shagging monkey programme. He didn't believe me. A couple of hours later and slightly the worse for wear, I looked around the pub. Most of the gang were trying their best to shag the girls. One boy was sitting in a tree playing with himself and another was asking a table of teenagers if they would like to see his banana. I turned to Gary and said, 'If I ever write a book it will be called *The Tale of the Shagging Monkeys*.' And that was that.

So there I was, weeks later, sitting in my car on the M4 with nothing to do. I reached across and pulled some paper and a pen out of my computer bag. I wrote the now infamous title on top of the paper. All the stress and anger flowed out of me. I suddenly didn't care where I was. It felt really strange. By the time the accident cleared hours later, I had the outline of the book already done. I'd created the main character and roughly completed two entire chapters. I didn't know where the hell it had come from. Words just poured from me.

Although I got home late, I felt so alive. I had the rest of the Chinese takeaway they had ordered and cracked open a bottle of red. I put my feet up and continued writing, hour after hour. My wife thought I had gone mad, well, madder than normal.

Within two months I had something which resembled a book. I didn't know anything about publishing or agents or the book world. I published it myself. Although, the spelling was terrible, the grammar even worse, surprisingly it made people laugh and got a four-star rating in the main Welsh newspaper, the *Western Mail*.

Chuffed, I turned up at one business review with a pile of shagging monkey books and handed them out to everyone. I hadn't told anyone I was writing it. The feedback was great from them. To be fair, The 5-Star Gimp was the first to tell me how much he enjoyed it. I bet he bloody did!!

9

Howling at the USSR

IF YOU EVER get the opportunity to travel to the old Eastern European Bloc countries, I suggest you don't watch the horror film *Hostel* a week before you head out. In the movie, supposedly based on a true story, unsuspecting Western tourists get kidnapped and tortured for fun.

Real or urban myth, I convinced myself it would be me getting drugged and waking up tied to a chair with some fat, consultant-hating, rich Russian businessman about to ram a flip chart marker pen into my eyeball.

But what could I do? I couldn't tell The Master I wasn't going to Moscow because of a film, or he would have rammed a ten-inch, extra thick and ribbed flip chart marker in my eyeball, sideways. Therefore, with visa in hand, I waited in my house for the taxi to take me to the airport.

Whenever we flew from Heathrow, we usually got a taxi to take us there and bring us back. It took some of the stress of airport travel out of the equation. On the negative side it often meant making small talk with some dull taxi driver for hours on end.

For my trip to Russia, a new driver turned up at my home. My first thought was, 'Oh fuck, I hope he's not going to lay his life story on me.' He was an older guy than the others, well past retirement age. He had these Paul Newman eyes, where the top lid drooped down over the corner of his eyelids.

Thankfully, he didn't do small talk either. That suited me fine.

It was still very early in the morning when we crossed the Severn Bridge, my flight wasn't scheduled to take off until after

11 a.m. I'm useless at trying to do any writing in a car. I get car sick. I sat, eyes closed, thinking of ideas for a new book. I must have actually dozed a little when, after about twenty minutes or so, I opened my eyes. 'Arrgggghhh,' I screamed.

The driver had fallen asleep, or looked like he had. I stiffened up in the back seat. He jumped, eyes now wide open. Our car nearly swerved into the central reservation.

I screamed again.

He swerved the other way.

'What's the matter?' he glared at me in the rear view mirror.

'Oh... nothing,' I lied.

My heartbeat like a bee's wing. Did I imagine it? Had I actually fallen asleep and dreamt he had fallen asleep? Maybe I had. I closed my eyes again. I waited a few minutes, then like a cartoon character, I sneaked open my one eye. I screamed again, only louder. He was sleeping like a baby. It hadn't been a dream. It was like the scene from *Father Ted* when the three priests all fell fast asleep in the moving car.

My driver jumped again. The car nearly went off the road again. He asked me the same question again, but more aggressively. I gave him the same reply again, but even more aggressively. My stress-free taxi journey had suddenly turned into a stressful nightmare. For the next two hours, I sat white-knuckled in the back, staring, unblinkingly at his reflection in the rear view mirror. Every now and again he caught me doing it. I'm sure he thought I was either mentally insane, or I fancied him.

I have never been so happy to get to an airport in my life. And at least I was flying Virgin and not AirFlock, or Air-only-one-wing, or whatever some of the other Eastern European airlines are called. For starters I didn't fancy pushing the plane down the runway and then being force-fed a meal of live worms and cold chips.

As we flew over Russia, I never realised just how much wooded area covered the country. We flew for hours over hundreds and hundreds of miles of thick forest. I wondered what could be down there, lurking in the undergrowth. I pictured generations of in-bred families living in huts with three-headed goats, or one-eyed children (or the other way around). The Russian version of *Texas Chain Saw Massacre*, re-titled the 'Kiev Pitch Fork Slaughter', with a thinner-looking Leatherface hanging thin-faced peasants up on meat hooks.

Now, I always thought the airport security at Cardiff airport were the most miserable son-of-bitch creatures God had ever put breath into. I was wrong. Compared to what greeted me at Moscow airport, the Cardiff bunch seemed more like the Tellytubbies.

Pete, my colleague, and I waited in the queue to go through passport control. Pete had been there a week before to plan out the workshop with the client. He knew the routine. Just before I walked the dreaded yellow line to show my passport, he whispered, 'Whatever you do, don't laugh.'

'Why? What?'

Too late. The bearded woman in the little glass cubicle motioned me towards her. I gulped and walked on. Why did he say that? Was she going to tell me a joke? Or tickle me with a huge ostrich feather? The closer I got, the bigger she got, and the smaller the cubicle got. It was as if the entire Russian army had squashed an elephant into a mini car. Her head filled it. I'm positive if she sneezed, or trumped, the whole cubicle would have blown to smithereens. (Now that would have made me laugh.)

I knew Pete was watching me, waiting for me to slip up.

I handed my passport over to Hairy Mary. Her hands like huge gorilla-paws. With a frown on her face she studied it and studied it, and studied it. A full ten minutes she stared at it for. She looked at the photo, then at me. She turned it ninety degrees and stared. I pondered if I should rotate ninety degrees as well to make it easier for her. I thought I'd better not.

At one point, she turned the passport completely upside down. She stared at me again. I glanced back at Pete. His shoulders jigged up and down. He could have given me more notice. The twat. I concentrated hard not to smile, but my lips developed a life of their own. I could feel them curling up at the ends. If I wasn't careful I would be standing there grinning like the Joker from *Batman*. Then fuck knows what would happen.

'Don't laugh,' I told myself. 'Don't laugh.' I thought of as many bad things as I could. Brussels sprouts, my mother-in-law (only joking), comedy programmes on ITV, traffic jams, getting imprisoned in Russia for ten years. The last one did the trick.

She finally handed it back to me and growled. I nodded and quickly hurried away.

'What the fuck was that all about?' I said to Pete while we waited for our luggage.

'She fancied you,' he joked. Well I hoped he was joking.

When we finally got out of the airport, the weather was exactly as I had imagined it to be. Two overcoats and a thick woollen vest colder than before we had boarded the plane in London. My first impression on driving away in our taxi was there was no way Russia had been a superpower. The place appeared so run down. Potholes littered the roads. It looked like the aftermath of a bombing raid during the war. And that was the main road to the major airport, in a major city. What's more, a train track sliced across the same road. We waited for ages while the longest freight train in the world hurtled by, full of coal and cattle. I couldn't imagine something like that happening in Heathrow or Gatwick, or even bloody Cardiff!

Most of the cars looked like they were held together by string and duct tape. The lorries were in a much worse condition. Windows cracked, bits hanging off or missing all together. There was definitely no MOT system here.

We left the city and drove out into the country. I don't want this to sound like I just made up a stereotypical image of Russia and added it to the book for effect, but every mile or so, as we drove, men staggered along the side of the road clutching bottles of white liquor. The drinking culture in the Welsh Valleys is bad, but this appeared to be on a different level altogether. God only knows what was in the bottles.

During our journey we passed a few police road blocks. Overweight, slobby-looking police officers stood by the side of the road flagging cars over.

'What are they looking for?' I asked the driver.

He told us the police randomly stopped cars on the premise of earning themselves a few bucks. 'If they stop us,' he warned, 'don't argue and just give them whatever they ask for.'

I glanced at Pete. The driver's words put a dampener on our already dampened mood. From then on, every time we came towards one of the road blocks, my heart stopped. We drove past about ten of them in total without getting pulled. Just as I thought we had escaped the pleasures of a mugging by the local constabulary, our car got waved over.

Our driver parked up. Two cops slowly walked towards us. Mad thoughts raced through my mind. What if they wanted all our money? What if they demanded two million pounds? Could we claim it back on expenses? Or would we need to ask them for a VAT receipt? What if they stripped us naked and left us go in the forest with the 'Kiev Pitch Fork Slaughter' gang who would definitely be waiting for us? What if they were gay and looking for a gobble? I wondered what Russian was for 'Oh, you've got such a pretty mouth, boy... open up wide!'

The younger of the two never took his eyes off us. They both carried guns that Arnie in the *Terminator* movie would have been proud of. Large batons and handcuffs were tucked into their belts. I swear one of them had a fist-shaped butt plug and a gimp mask around the back of his belt.

The younger cop asked me a direct question. I glanced at the taxi driver. Bravely he took hold of the conversation for me. I assumed he was explaining that we were out-of-towners. Jackpot signs lit up his eyes. He stroked the butt plug. They both nodded and walked around the car to the boot.

'Oh fuck,' Pete hissed to me, 'I have a pair of binoculars in my bag.'

'What?' I almost screamed out my reply. 'What the fuck have you got a pair of fucking binoculars in your fucking bag for, in fucking Russia?'

'To look at birds.'

'What?'

'I'm a bird watcher.'

'You're a fucking nutcase,' I hissed. I pictured us spending thirty years doing hard labour in some salt mine at the far tip of the country because he wanted to slyly look at some great grey tits.

Luckily, they didn't look through our luggage. After more conversation between our driver and the coppers, the driver shook his head.

'What?' I asked.

'They want two million pounds and a blow-job... each!' Well, I was sure that's what he said. I could have been wrong. Actually they demanded fifty quid from us and they would leave our honour intact.

Pete handed over the money before I had a chance to get mine out of my pocket. Maybe he was really a spy and he had more than binoculars in his bag. I didn't care; I just wanted to get out of there.

The police in my town had a bad reputation. Rumours of them jumping queues in fish and chip shops and demanding sausage in batter with extra chips, and then walking out without paying were commonplace. But this was intimidating, organised crime on a scary scale.

We didn't say a word for the next thirty minutes as we drove through several, small villages. The houses looked like a cat with an acute case of asthma, never mind a wolf could huff and puff and blow them down. Again, lots of drunken men staggered about.

'It must be giro-day,' I muttered.

The factory we were working in was situated on the edge of

a town famous for making fighter aeroplanes in the war. We drove past an actual plane positioned on a roundabout.

'If this trip gets any worse, I'm going to fly that bloody thing home!' I laughed.

'You will be OK when you see our hotel,' Pete gave me a weird kind of smirk. And no wonder. There was no nice, plush hotel. There wasn't even a hotel room. Just two tin sheds located in the factory grounds. Two metal caravans, with a tiny bedroom, tiny bathroom and a tiny lounge area with a tiny settee and a huge table.

Pete had already warned me the food was not the best. 'Fucking terrible,' he actually said.

And he wasn't wrong.

But being an old boy scout (well for four weeks) I came prepared. I smuggled into the country a couple of badass Peter's chicken pasties and a half-dozen Pot Noodles. On the plus side they sold strong beer for about 11p each in a small shop in between the tin sheds. We bought five pounds' worth and stocked up the fridge and the sink in my bathroom. Most nights, like a pair of diddycoy consultants, we sat in our tin huts sampling the simple pleasures of life. Pot Noodles, pasties, beers and a few chocolate bars courtesy of the company.

There were other perks. The women milling around the large office block where the training took place were drop-dead gorgeous. They didn't have any of the McDonald's blubber fat often found on Western girls these days. Or the misspelt tattoos like a few Welsh girls displayed with pride on their knuckles. These were stunning-looking creatures. Slim figures, high cheek bones and sexy, cat-like Eastern European eyes. The only downside was most of them dressed like women from the early Eighties. All shoulder pads, big hair and glitter.

Like two old perves, Pete and I would wander aimlessly through the office in between sessions pretending to go to the water fountain. Naturally we picked the one furthest away from the training room. Well, the water tasted better!

One English girl in our sessions had moved out there a year

or two before. A very knowledgeable and intelligent female destined to get to the top, whatever it took. She was always willing to stand up at the front and explain to everyone what was going on. Her actions proved an interesting addition because she had a little quirk. Or two, big quirks, actually. During one of her feedback sessions, two senior managers came in and sat at the back. I'm not sure if it was a power thing with her, or whether she just got turned on by being the centre of attention. As she talked, her nipples came to life. They stood erect through her white T-shirt like doorstops. The more she spoke and the more management words she used, the bigger they got. I couldn't take my eyes off them. Fuck me, if The Prof had been in the room and started spouting out all of his consultant bullshit words, her chest would have probably exploded and covered us all in titty stuff.

I looked at Pete. His tongue hung out like a bloke who had walked through the desert without water for forty days and nights. As soon as she sat down again, disappointingly, her doorstops shrank back to normal size. Being two, old, wiry creatures, we made sure she fed back as much as possible using as many consultant buzzwords as we could squeeze in. I think we even made some up.

Late one night, I sat alone in my tiny lounge area in my tin shack doing some writing. All the lights were off except for a small lamp by my side. We'd sunk a few beers and a chicken and mushroom Pot Noodle earlier.

Suddenly, I felt something land on me. I brushed it away and carried on. Then something else fell on my head, then again. I leapt up and switched the main light on. Ants! Armies of them dropping down from the ceiling above me. I went into a killing frenzy. I slaughtered a million of them but still they came, parachuting down on me. They regrouped by the leg on the table and attacked in one big mass. They forced me to retreat into my bedroom. I barricaded myself in. I put sheets under the door. I lay in bed scratching and listening out for them. Every time I almost dropped off to sleep I could hear them planning to sneak into my room and carry me away like a discarded half-eaten sandwich from a picnic in the park.

The next morning I looked like death warmed up.

'What's happened to you?' Pete asked.

'Ants,' I replied

'Ants?'

'Yes... stop saying the word. Fucking ants... armies of them.'

I had another two nights fighting an unwinnable war with the insects. I even asked someone if there was a zoo nearby where I could hire an anteater by the hour. They couldn't understand me. In the end I just bought the insects some sandwiches from the canteen. I left them in the corner of the lounge. The next morning the sandwiches hadn't been touched.

'I told you the food was shit,' Pete reminded me when I told him.

*

When I got home to Wales I was shattered and miserable. Russia had been an experience I had done and never wanted to do again. I was just getting over the experience when my next assignment took me to another cold and grey Eastern European place, darkest Hungary.

Balasz still remains the coolest bloke I've ever met. If James Bond had been Hungarian, Balasz would have been him. Balasz... James Balasz or whatever his first name was. He never told me. Dark and extremely handsome with Romany gypsy features, he spoke at least six different languages. Still only twenty-eight years of age, he smoked each cigarette like it was the last cigarette of his life. He made love to it. He savoured every drag, right down to his fingernails.

He picked me up from Budapest airport well after 9 p.m. one Sunday night. The city looked like a brilliant contrast of lifestyles as we drove through it. The rich and poor, the business and the creative world, all mingled into a dark, broody, gloomy place. Slogans and graffiti littered the walls. The kind of place I imagined a good photographer having multiple orgasms every time he focused his lens.

Before we left the city Balasz stopped at a small eatery. Everyone knew him: Bar owners, diners, prostitutes, fruit salesmen, beggar kids on the street. He seemed so popular I half-expected to see his face on the back of their money. The food and wine were fantastic.

Another consultant who had been to the city told me he couldn't get over the amount of prostitutes lining the streets at night. 'They get uglier the further out of the city you go,' he added.

And he was right. As we drove I saw some of the nicest-looking girls I'd seen anywhere in the world. By the time we were on the open road they got, let's just say, a little plainer. A mile out they were dog rough. Real double baggers. One sat in a wheelchair. Another old woman with no teeth, held a pig under her arm. I wasn't sure if she was a hooker or a farmer's wife (probably both). I wondered if the pig was part of the deal.

After a long, two-hour journey we arrived at a small industrial town next to a wide, fast-flowing river. Balasz hadn't said much during the journey, happy just to puff away on at least sixty last cigarettes of his young life. I smelt like a chimney by the time we arrived at the small, family-owned hotel.

The diminutive, round-shouldered, hundred-and-thirty-year-old owner showed me to my room. To say it was basic would have been an overstatement. Everything in the room was made of wood, even the light shades. The low-lying wooden bed almost touched the floor. It looked like something Goldilocks would have climbed into and still said, 'what the fuck is all this about?'

The man grinned and left. I threw my case onto the bed in anger.

'Five days of sleeping in this badly-made sauna,' I muttered.

Outside the window, I saw a man's body floating down the fast-flowing river. Well it looked like a man's body; it could have been a log or a crocodile. Did they have crocodiles in Hungary? Or men-shaped logs? Or men-shaped crocodiles? I was thoroughly pissed off.

Suddenly, the old man came rushing back in. 'Sorry, sorry... wrong room, wrong room.' He grinned wider. 'Me... me... you follow.'

I knew there must have been a mistake. I was consultant royalty. I followed him two rooms down.

'This one... this one,' he muttered.

I walked in all cocky-like. My face dropped. It was exactly the same as the other one. No difference whatsoever! It even had a lopsided cupboard. I looked out at the body floating down the river; I wished it was me.

Next morning Balasz picked me up bright and early. He gave the impression he hadn't been to bed. Jokingly, I mentioned it to him. He shrugged, took a long drag on his fag and drove us towards the medium-sized car manufacturing plant.

The session took place in a cramped, muggy and noisy training room located above the welding section. It felt so hot, beads of sweat rolled down the walls. Ten guys sat around a table waiting for us. I introduced myself. They stared back at me blankly. They looked across at Balasz. He said something in Hungarian. They all nodded.

'Do you all know why we are here?' I asked them my standard opening question.

Again they stared at me. Balasz spoke up again. Then it hit me. None of them spoke English, except for the words 'Manchester United' and 'Ryan Giggs'. Well, at least he was Welsh.

What was it with me and non-English speaking people? It was becoming a running fucking joke.

I continued rambling on like an idiot. They looked at me as if I was an idiot, then at Balasz, who they looked at as if he was a king. He talked in Hungarian. They nodded in a strange Hungarian sort of way, heads cocked to one side. This continued for ages. One time they all burst out laughing at something he said. They sat rocking back and forth on their seats. Balasz looked at me and shrugged. I could see the devil dancing about in his eyes.

The problems with this two-way method of getting my point across was it took three times longer to get my point across. Between the language difference and the cigarette breaks Balasz told me they insisted on having, we were way behind schedule, and we had just only started.

After a lunch of odd-looking slimy sandwiches and lumps of even stranger-looking meat, Balasz suggested he ran the session completely. I hesitated, knowing he was still in his training and I was supposed to be in charge. But, we needed to do something different. I agreed. So I sat in the corner, helpless, while Balasz, the cool spy, took complete control of my session. I didn't understand a word he was saying. He could have been telling them about the twin sisters he poked the night before for all I knew, but by then I didn't care. Between the lack of air conditioning and the smell of BO and bad breath, I just wanted it to finish as fast as we could.

At the time I was in the middle of writing a book, and was looking for a good name for an evil, banana spider emperor. After getting Balasz's permission, my evil character was complete.

All-in-all, another strange week but, in truth, everything turned out just fine. I should never have doubted it from the super cool Hungarian. And it wasn't the last time our paths crossed.

I actually like Germans.

When I watch a football match between a British and a German side, it's always a full-bodied, take no prisoners affair. No diving, or crying, or stupid goal celebrations. Our nations, I think, are pretty much the same, with the same 'don't take any shit' attitude.

All right, before going on, let me rephrase that. I like most Germans. Mathias was actually one German I disliked... a lot.

The global company Balasz worked for wanted to train more staff at other sites. Consequently I got the gig to run a Lean coach programme for the business in a number of sites across Europe. The first week-long session took place in Newport, south Wales. An added bonus for me, because it was close to home.

Newport is known for three things. A transporter bridge, a rap group called Goldie Looking Chain, and a spoof song about how bad the place is. That's basically it. So I wondered what the group of individuals flying in from Europe would make of it. There were six delegates from the UK, five from Germany and Mr Balasz, the good-looking prince of Hungary.

The format of the workshop was similar to others I had done, only difference being, in this one, I had to remember 'not to mention the war!' A lot easier said than done when Mathias the Fascist, goose-stepped into the room like Hitler's nephew. He even had the same hairstyle combed to the side, but a slightly bigger moustache. He glanced around the room and shook his head violently. He stared at the seating arrangements and shook his head. He then glared at me and shook his head.

I wanted to knock his fucking head clean off his shoulders and he hadn't said a word yet. I could just tell he was going to be a boil on the end of my nose. It didn't get any better when I started the session. Everything I said he jumped straight in there, guns blazing. 'We don't do it like that in Germany. We do it much better.' On, and on, and on, he droned.

'Well you don't do fucking world wars better. Do you?' I wanted to blurt back but I had been warned. I could have plumped for, 'What about the 1966 World Cup?' But since the Krauts had won about forty World Cups since that time, I thought I better let that old, sleeping, football dog lie.

At lunchtime, a typical British factory buffet got wheeled out. Plates full of scotch eggs, sausage rolls and all the other usual suspects. I have never seen grown men looking so scared at a pasty cut in half in my life, as the five Germans did as they stood around the plate.

'What is zat?' one of them asked.

Mathias rubbed his chin and, of course, shook his head.

'A pasty,' one of the Welsh guys said. 'Don't you have pasties in Germany?'

Mathias piped up, 'No, no, no... we have much better food in Germany than that. Wait until you come to our site in three weeks.'

If I had been sharper, I should have hit back with some witty comment. But I couldn't think of anything. Perhaps I should have just hit him with the bloody pasty.

After lunch we walked around the site in one big group. I'd asked them to make notes of what they thought the place was like from a Lean perspective.

I must admit, the factory wasn't the best steel mill I had ever seen. In fact, it wouldn't have been the best steel mill next to one which had been bombed flat in the war. See, I couldn't stop thinking of war references. The place looked dreadful. Big chunks of cladding on the main walls were missing, allowing the wind, with a chip on its shoulder, to come whizzing through every bone in our bodies. Every area looked untidy and dirty. Gangs of operators stood about drinking tea from dirty mugs and not doing anything constructive.

Other than that, it wasn't too bad!

Back at the room Mathias came out firing on all cylinders. By the end of his rant, which included six 'Wait until you come to our plant' and at least ten 'We are the superior race' and some other shit, he'd pissed off every non-German in the building. Even the cool Balasz lost his cool. He snarled before storming out for a cigarette.

I managed to get through the week without the warring factions digging trenches at either end of the training room and chucking hand-grenades, or stale pasties at each other. But only just.

Round two took place three weeks later, not far from Frankfurt. A taxi dropped me off in a small, quaint, German town just after midnight. I tried the door to the small boarding house where I was staying.

It was locked. I knocked. No one answered. I knocked several more times. No one came. I stood outside with my computer bag, my suitcase and a couple of extra bags with some exercises needed for the sessions.

Still nothing.

I didn't know what I was going to do. I bet Mathias had planned it, I told myself. Maybe he was filming it for the German version of *You've Been Framed* – 'Zou've Been Fucked, Consultant Boy!'

Then I saw the smallest of signs in the window telling all guests the keys for the rooms were in a box outside the pub up the street. I raced up the cobbled street and finally got into my room.

With German efficiency, the taxi picking me up appeared outside at exactly five past seven as stated. When I got to the training room, Mathias sat there waiting. This was his territory now. His battlefield. The other British guys, except one, were staying five miles away in a different town.

The tour of the plant, I must say, was better than the one in Newport. But with my trained eye I could see lots of opportunities for improvement.

At lunchtime, Mathias cattle-marched us to the factory canteen. The way he puffed out his chest with pride I thought we were going to eat at a five-star restaurant. The food in my opinion was awful. Plates full of sauerkraut (pickled cabbage) and some kind of sausage that looked and tasted like a large dog's cock. Give me out-of-date pasties any time.

Politely I smiled and told them how nice it was. I wasn't a complete fool; these guys were still paying my wages.

The British sales guy staying in my hotel offered to drive

me to work the next morning instead of me going in a taxi. Later that night, after a few beers he told me how he hated the business and how he couldn't wait to leave. He then proceeded to get thoroughly pissed.

When my alarm went off in the morning I hurried outside to wait for him. He didn't show. With time moving on, I tried calling him several times. His mobile went straight to answer machine. Shit, I was stuck. Out of the twenty-five rooms in the reception-less hotel I didn't know which one he was in. I frantically called him again on the phone. Still nothing. I had no option but to buzz each intercom to find the bastard. A few unhappy Germans answered. Then I heard a British voice.

'Steve is that you?'

'Uhmmmm.'

'Steve… come on… we're fucking late.'

The intercom went dead. Two minutes later, Steve rushed out of the door. His eyes like piss holes in the snow.

When we got to the factory forty-five minutes late, Mathias stood by the window, deliberately shaking his head. I tried to explain but gave up. There wasn't any point. One-nil to the German.

On the Wednesday night, after a meal and a tour around a German castle, all the Brits and Balasz went for a nightcap in a pub. With Mathias nowhere in sight, and with the help of some very strong lager, we let our hair down in the quiet bar.

An hour or so later, I ambled back from the toilet and noticed two youths, in their early twenties, skulking in the corner. Both with 1970s skinhead haircuts, they appeared to be staring at our table. With my Merthyr instincts fully engaged, I kept my eye on them.

A couple more similar-looking youths showed up. They sat sipping their beers and whispering to each other. Maybe they were just out for a beer, not out for trouble. Then it all kicked off.

Balasz walked back from the bar carrying a tray of drinks. One of the skinheads purposely barged into him, knocking the drinks over the floor. Without hesitation us Brits jumped to our feet and raced over, bottles in hand.

'All for one and one for all,' our battle cry.

Both gangs stood, glowering at each other. I, for one, was shitting myself. I think the others were too, but we must have put on a brave face. The skinhead opposite me looked a right mean bastard. On saying that, have you ever seen a soft-looking skinhead? They are all mean-looking bastards. My instinct told me to smash him first, yet my head told me to run like fuck. I hadn't had a rumble since I was fourteen, in a park in my town, against the Protestants. It wasn't a Catholic versus Protestants, religious thing. It was one of their girls fancied my mate thing.

The barman, a rugged, thickset man, shoved his way in between us. He held a tasty baseball bat in his large hands. He didn't look at us. He just stared at his own countrymen. He yelled out something in German to the biggest of them. The youth huffed and puffed and puffed some more, but didn't back down. My heart was pumping. I thought, 'Fucking hell I'm only over here to run a fucking workshop, not fight with Hitler's youth.'

The tension was unbelievable. The barman poked the big youth in the chest with the bat. Thankfully, the skinheads backed down and left.

I was physically shaking where I stood. So scared, I could hardly talk. When we were sure they weren't going to run back in and batter us, we started high-fiving each other. We may have been good at our jobs, but I bet we would have been shit fighters. The barman knew that as well and phoned taxis for us. We agreed not to mention our near-war experience to Mathias or the others.

Thursday was the day we all analysed the work done so far. Even in very friendly companies, it could be a really tough day. A session where the group challenged what the host company did and suggested improvements. That Thursday was without doubt the hardest I have ever encountered, before or since. Within twenty minutes it turned into Germany versus the rest of the world. The Germans, led by Adolf Mathias, the rest of the world marshalled by me, Winston Bunko.

Everything we challenged, Mathias counter-challenged. Whenever anyone suggested something, he shot it down in flames without giving it a chance. The Red Baron he should have been called.

He had an excuse for everything and he took it all too personally. I didn't. The team didn't. We wanted the best for the business. It got embarrassing. I needed to do something and quickly. Maybe a game of football on Christmas Day in no-man's-land would have broken the ice, or his neck. I remember the lesson I had learnt from Tom all those years before. I called a coffee break.

'We just had one,' someone replied.

'Out, everyone,' I said firmly, 'except you.' I pointed at Mathias.

No one rushed to move. They all wanted to stay. When they had gone, me and the German squared up to each other like two gunfighters in Dodge City.

'What the hell you playing at, Mathias?' He folded his arms and shook his head. 'You shake your head again and I'll knock it fucking off.' I lost it. I even poked him in the chest. 'Look, if the place is so good why the hell have your management team insisted we do the activity here?'

He came back with some crap about how we had bombed his uncle's cake shop in Dresden in the war and how Anne Frank wasn't really a young girl but a fifty-five-year-old hooker called Debbie, or something along these lines. I wasn't really listening by then.

'This is not a war,' I almost screamed at him. 'It's not Britain versus Germany. Everyone here is here to help you. Not fight against you.'

His eyes burnt into my skin. I honestly thought, we would end up scrapping. I hoped he wasn't hard. I pictured him knocking me out and then strutting out of the room, bloodied hands above his head, announcing that he was 'Ze Daddy'.

But what if I beat him? What the hell would I do then? Hide! Run for the border!

Then, to be fair, he held out his hand. 'I'm sorry,' he muttered.

I shook it. 'Let's go and have a coffee and then let's get this sorted,' I added.

Mathias improved a lot after that. He still had his 'let's roll the tanks into Poland' moments now and again, but we ended up with quite a good result in the end.

I learnt a lot from that trip.

Never let things fester. Always get things out in the open, and never stand opposite the biggest skinhead bastard when there's a possible bar brawl about to take place.

10

The Massacre at Hereford Mount

AFTER SAMPLING THE deadly delights of Europe, I found things closer to home just as unpredictable.

During my short time in the business I had already been on some wild goose-chases. However, nothing compared to the workshop I ran in Warrington with Joe. The event took place in a plush office block within its own grounds. The scenery was absolutely picturesque: stunning, well-maintained gardens surrounded a beautiful lake.

One lunchtime, to clear the old 'too many glasses of wine the night before' cobwebs away, Joe and I took a stroll around the grounds. It had been raining badly but it had stopped to allow the sun to come out.

As we walked near the lake, a loud squawking noise rose up behind us. Startled, I turned around. There, looking straight at us was a goose. And not just any old goose. The Arnold Schwarzenegger of geese. A muscle-bound creature with murder in its eyes and a beak as big as its 'fuck-off' attitude.

We carried on walking. The bird kept coming. I'm not sure if it thought we were going to nick its eggs, or were a threat to its chicks or if it was just blind drunk and looking for a rumble.

Our pace quickened. It flapped harder behind us. With its wingspan well over six foot wide, it looked like an insane, albino, prehistoric beast.

Without saying a word, we both ran. Lucky for me, the killer goose focused on Joe. I climbed up on a bench like a girl who just saw a huge spider.

Joe tried to leg it up the small grassy mound. But his shoes and the wet grass were a slippery combination. The harder he ran, the further away he didn't actually get. He just slid back down very slowly. The goose snapped at his heels. It ended up like the scene out of *Jaws* when Quint, the shark hunter, slid off the sinking boat kicking and screaming into the hungry mouth of the nasty fish. I'm not sure if the goose could have eaten Joe in one sitting. Maybe it intended to drag him back to the island on the lake, and get some feathery mates around for a human-style BBQ later.

I was too scared to laugh and too afraid to help him. Joe kicked it. The goose shrieked. It flew up and tried to surprise Joe with a head-peck. Joe ducked just in time. A fight to the death ensued. The bird pecking, Joe's fists lunging. I'm not sure if someone could get imprisoned for killing a goose, but it would have made a great news report that night.

Then surprisingly, with Joe struggling to breathe, the creature hissed one last time before waddling away.

'What the fuck got into him?' I started laughing at the bird ambush.

Joe leaned on the bench, his hand bleeding. 'It was like that bastard whippet. But at least no one saw us...' he stopped short. Up in the office block, a line of hysterical faces stared down at us. Thank God no one had recorded it on their mobiles.

The 'last of the geese wrestlers' and the 'Taffy goose slayers' were just two of the comments we had to put up with for the rest of the week.

On the subject of getting attacked by strange flying creatures, I once ran a workshop in an agricultural college in mid-Wales. The entire place smelt of manure and Madras curry. I didn't know if there was a link.

It was so hot all the windows in the room were wide open. Every now and again, I noticed a few flies buzzing about the room. Nothing unusual, just a couple of them near the windowsill. I carried on talking.

Suddenly, a girl screamed. I looked around and I'm not

exaggerating when I say that at least twenty million of the little critters flew through the windows at us. We were under attack. They swooped down, a thick bluebottle duvet coming towards us, looking for blood, or whatever bluebottles look for. Fighting them off with a roll of paper, we scrambled outside. I phoned reception. An old guy appeared five minutes later holding a tiny can of fly spray and a fly-squasher.

'In there,' I almost laughed as I pointed.

He slowly opened the door. 'Bloody hell... that doesn't look good,' he said and sprinted off. 'I'll be back,' he added.

I pictured him returning like the *Terminator* (the Fly-minator) carrying a flame thrower, or the biggest spider in the world. I shivered. Flies I could cope with, spiders I hated with a passion. In fact, he never came back.

In the end we moved rooms.

Internally, within our business, lots of dramatic changes took place. Sales climbed steeply and we grew bigger each day. More people clambered onboard the BS Consulting shuttle bus heading to the Promised Land. This meant the old strategy of just employing forty-year-old white, beer-bellied, metal-heads had to change.

'It's time to diversify,' The 5-Star Gimp sent out an email.

And diversify we did, with some spectacular failures.

*

During an internal training day, out of the mist, the shape of a woman appeared. Late thirties, and as Tom muttered to me, 'with a face that looked like it had been beaten with a wok in a fight to the death in a paddy field, and the personality of yesterday's cabbage.'

She'd studied at one of the top universities in the UK. A place of such importance and bullshit that apparently delegates needed heads the size of go-carts and egos to match to get accepted there.

That morning she'd introduced herself, followed by a long list of letters after her name. I'm positive the letters spelt the words 'COMPLETE NUTCASE'. She may have acted like a brainy bird, but to me she seemed to have as much commonsense as a young, drunken, English teenager on his first piss-up trip to Magaluf. A plastic University Guru with little real experience of working in the real world with real people. As expected, the other partners raved about how great she was. In their eyes she was the eighth Wonder Woman of the World. To many others she was the Emperor's New Clothes, bought from Oxfam.

Every meeting she turned up to, she basically took over. I think she loved the sound of her own voice. She poetically strung long sentences together. I, for one, didn't have a clue what she was bleating on about. Most of us were glad when she disappeared for a while to have a baby. But, like a bad smell, she returned months later during a review meeting.

I'm sorry to say but the mere sight of her sent a shiver through me like a cold draught on a summer's day.

What's more, like an eccentric female kangaroo, she had her four-month-old sprog strapped to her chest. I assumed the sprog's name would be something kooky like King Henry Tarquin Jackson the Thud or something. I don't think I was far wrong.

An hour into the review, Tom stood up to give a short presentation on what was happening in the Welsh market.

'Can I ask a question?' brainy woman asked.

Rolling my eyes, I glanced across at her. 'What the hell...?' My mouth fell open. She only had her left breast out and King Henry was sucking away on her nipple like a good 'un. Everyone sat staring in disbelief. She didn't bat an eyelash. Not a hint of embarrassment on her face. I know it's only natural, and she shouldn't have to be embarrassed, but surely there was a time and place for that sort of thing? And that time and place wasn't when Tom was telling us about accessing European funding. He was nervous enough as it was. He completely lost his trail of thought. Sweat dripped off his head and nearly fused the overhead projector.

Then the noise hit me. The sound of the baby sucking will stay with me forever. It sounded as if a pack of zombies were eating the intestines of a fat policeman in a small greenhouse. It was horrendous.

It became obvious she was making a point with the whole breastfeeding extravaganza. An 'I'm a woman, I have breasts and if King Henry wants a pint of mammy's brainy milk, then he's going to get it' kind of point.

As the flesh-eating zombie kid munched noisily on her boob, she continued with her question. No-one knew what the fuck she said. All eyes were transfixed on the kid and the mammary gland. Even The Prof sat lost for words. He moved his chair away. I'm sure The Glass Is Always Half Full partner had a boner! The 5-Star Gimp dribbled coffee all down his chin.

So, with the business becoming more perverse, no, sorry, diverse, everyone needed to change their mindset and carry on. It took some getting used to, though.

*

Christmas was the time of year for us all to chill out and pat ourselves on the back for being so wonderful. A three-day BIG business review cum piss-up, was always arranged the week before Christmas.

The one event at Cardiff Bay took some beating. First off, while having a team dinner at a fancy Spanish restaurant, Joe clumsily fell back off his chair and smashed the biggest terracotta plant pot in the entire world. We had to fork out two hundred and twenty quid before the machete-wielding restaurant owners let us go.

After that, we went to a nightclub where The Trainspotter got thrown head-first out of the disco by some mean-looking bouncers. Out of his tree on cider, he had squeezed some girl's arse on the dance floor. Of course none of us rushed over to stick up for him. Sometimes, even friendly and unassuming trainspotters needed to find out for themselves how tough life could be.

At around 1 a.m., a gang of us sauntered back towards the hotel. Out of the blue, Tom screamed and fell to the floor as if he'd been shot. Thing was, he had been shot.

A car sped off with a boy hanging out of the passenger window holding a slug gun.

'I've been shot,' Tom moaned.

As quick as a flash, I said. 'It looked like the MD from St Davids.'

'Fuck off, you cunt,' Tom yelled back at me. 'This is serious.'

The boys in the car must have thought they had brought down a rhinoceros. I imagined them going home to a council flat in Ely, smoking a joint, eating some HobNobs and then settling down to watch the drive-by shooting on their mobiles.

Tom was too proud to take my offer of a hand up. 'Fuck off, you piss-taking wanker,' he spat. He clambered up and bounded after the car for a few strides.

The morning after, The Trainspotter sat rather sheepishly at the back of the room, his glasses held together by a piece of clear Sellotape. He had a black eye and a swollen lip. But the biggest cheer went up when Tom the Terminator hobbled in.

'Do you need a cushion to sit on?' someone muttered.

We could be a cruel bunch of bastards at times.

Every year we did a Secret Santa. It's a game where a person gets secretly picked to buy a gift of £10 for someone else in the business. I quite liked it 'cos it made me think about the individual I had got paired with. If I hadn't worked with them, it made me go out of my way to talk to others to find out what he, or she, had done over the past year.

The 5-Star Gimp didn't get the concept of it at all. I think he felt things like this were trivial and below him. So every year he gave the same gift to whoever he had been drawn with. He always bought them an A to Z road atlas of the UK purchased from the garage as he drove to the event.

During these Xmas events, the business usually invited possible recruits to come along and see what we were all about. One possible newcomer was a very nice and pleasant Asian woman in her mid-fifties. A human resource specialist and not the woman from the takeaway down the road, as Joe commented as she walked in.

By mid-morning, the Secret Santa was in full flow. The 5-Star Gimp had just handed Tom a brand new hot-off-the-press copy of the A to Z atlas of the UK. Tom's face was a picture.

Next up, The 1970s Porn Star handed over his well-wrapped present to one of the office girls. Oddly for him, he went bright red and told her to open it later.

'No way,' everyone shrieked. Even The 5-Star Gimp yelled out. (He could be a cheeky twat with skin like a fucking rhino on times.)

The girl opened the box and pulled out a plastic Santa Claus. Not just any old Santa, mind you. A singing Elvis Santa. And not just any old singing Elvis Santa, no it had to be a Pakistani singing Elvis Santa.

Without thinking anything was wrong, the girl switched it on. It started singing an Elvis song with a Pakistani accent and jiggling its hips about. Everyone stared at the singing plastic toy, then at the possible new, Asian recruit, then back at the doll. The office girl sat, too shocked to turn it off. No one said a word. The place shrouded in a deadly silence, except for the warblings of 'Santa Claus is Comin' to Town' in a rock and roll Pakistani accent. Thirty-five, mature, so-called intelligent people sat there, dying to laugh but too mature and so-called intelligent to do so. It was stupid and childish but priceless.

Fortunately, the all-singing, all-dancing Pakistani Elvis finally stopped singing and jigging about. Everyone breathed out a collective sigh of relief. But then lightning struck for the second time. Oh yes... just before The Prof introduced the next Secret Santa presentation, the singing Pakistani Elvis started up again with an encore. Full blast, dancing and singing as if someone had just rammed four new Duracells up his battery flap.

My sides hurt. Tears rolled down my face. Joe, sitting next to me, spat tea out over the table. The liquid even came out of his nose and ears.

'Will someone shut that bloody thing up,' The Glass Is Always Half Full partner, for once, lost his cool.

Joe jumped up and took it away.

'Sorry,' The Porn Star said to the Asian woman.

'Sorry,' everyone else mouthed at the Asian woman.

'That's OK,' she muttered through clenched teeth.

She never did join our business.

*

The bizarre behaviour of the Tit-Woman wasn't the only weirdo in the business to make my blood boil. We began employing some right oddballs. None came odder or stranger than Rambo Roberts.

In my humble opinion, Rambo Roberts had no right being a consultant in the first place. He lacked personality and any basic understanding of how to communicate with people. A fifty-five-year-old, silver-haired, ex-soldier with enough baggage on his shoulders to sink the *Titanic*.

His main weakness: Having no consultant intervention skills at all.

His main strength: Slicing someone's throat with a cheese wire on the Brecon Beacons at midnight.

I first crossed paintballs with him during a team-building event on a cold day in Hereford. I'd seen him a few times but never had anything to do with him until that day.

In the same breath, I had never done paintballing before and was actually looking forward to it. Naively, I thought it wouldn't hurt and it would be a laugh. I assumed we would be well padded up and the paintballs would be harmless, like small, water balloons.

How bloody wrong could I be? It wasn't a laugh at all and it was very, very painful. The pain lasted for days. The mental scars never really faded away.

The battle took place in a big field surrounded by trees, trenches and the odd empty building or two. On the day, a gang of students from some local university were also having a fun paintball day out. All bright eyed, bushy tailed in ripped jeans and sticky-up hair, they ambled off to do their own thing.

The organisers called the first event 'grab the flag'. A bit like football, we split into two teams. The winners would be the team to grab the flag from the other team's goals. Keeping to the sport analogy, when I played football as a youngster I played full back. I wasn't interested in being the one scoring all the goals up front. A good full back was worth his weight in gold.

With that in mind, I positioned myself near our flag. I hid down in a little, grassy bunker. I waited, while the others raced about like fools wanting to be the heroes. My aim was to protect our flag like I protected our goalkeeper many years before. Only thing was, my team of soldiers were not Manchester United. They weren't even Newport fucking County. They were useless, dropping like splattered flies. I stayed undercover.

Up on the flank, I saw Rambo Roberts, the enemy, sneaking among the trees. The trees which we had been told were off limits several times by the organisers at the start. He couldn't see me. I could see the grin on his face as he closed in on our flag.

'I'll have you, you cheating Rambo bastard,' I whispered.

Bang... Bang... Bang.

I nailed him with everything I had. But instead of falling down dead, he raced off in the bushes.

'Oy... I killed you,' I yelled.

'No you didn't,' he shouted back. 'You missed.'

'I fucking didn't.' I looked up from my hole. 'I fucking hit you...'

Booosh.

125

I got shot right in the forehead by someone else. Fucking hell, it hurt like hell. I put my hands up straight away.

How proper soldiers do that for real is beyond me. How they can just lay in a trench knowing that at any moment they could get their heads blown off must be really bloody scary. I take my bobble hat off to them.

With the game lost, Rambo Roberts appeared out of the bushes, grinning like a Cheshire rat. Where he'd been shot by me, and many others, his overall resembled the colours of the rainbow. I glanced at him and shook my head. I took a deep dislike to him from that day onwards. I put him in my invisible book, along with Mathias and my dead careers officer.

The day got less fun and more painful with each activity we played. All the office girls got shot in the tits, which couldn't have been healthy at all. Pete got shot just above his eye when his goggles slipped off. An egg-shaped lump appeared on his forehead. But the biggest cheer of the day went up when Chris, the IT apprentice, got shot in the nuts.

As he rolled around in agony on the ground, Tom loomed over him. 'At least you won't be able to father any fucking kids,' he blurted.

Another loud cheer went up.

After lunch, the organisers told us the next exercise involved one group being housed up in a concrete bunker until the other group killed them all. The aim was to see which group could survive the longest, until they got wiped out.

'No way,' one of the girls piped up. 'My tits can't take any more.'

Although I didn't have any tits, I did have balls, so I fully agreed with her comments. That sounded stupid and pointless.

'I'll fucking wipe him out,' Tom grunted about the organiser.

If we had been miners we would have gone on strike. We told them we didn't want any of that nonsense. But then we showed our true colours. Backtracking, the organiser asked if we fancied a match-up against the students for the last battle of the day. Although black and bruised, we couldn't resist pitting our wits and management skills against the youth of today, who could possibility end up as the business consultants of tomorrow.

They say everything is equal in love and war. But, ashamedly, things definitely weren't equal in war that day and there's wasn't much love about either. We had one massive advantage over our enemy. In the cold light of day, the students were skint and couldn't afford much more ammunition. It had already been quite an expensive day out, especially when the organisers designed events for punters to use up bullets, and then buy more bullets.

We, on the other hand, were wealthy consultants on an all-expenses-paid team-building event. Bullets weren't a problem for us. Out came the credit cards. We bought as much ammunition as we could carry. We bought hand-grenades and missiles. We would have bought tanks and aeroplanes if they had been on offer.

'Let's do these commie bastards,' Rambo Roberts spread a line of mud across his nose like war paint.

The battle itself reminded me of watching scenes on TV of the American fighter pilots in Iraq cruising around in state-of-the-art jets with weapons of destruction dangling off their wings. Down below the Iraqis hid out in wooden huts made from orange boxes with a couple of pea shooters and handmade bows and arrows.

It was as one-sided as that.

Rambo Roberts turned into an absolute, mental warrior. But if I was honest, we all did. The poor students didn't stand a chance. They cowered in their trench in one big mass. We surrounded them, firing at will. Hate and years of pent-up anger in our eyes.

The next day, I not only woke up sore all over, but also feeling riddled with guilt. Guilt and embarrassment at my part in the massacre of the students at Hereford Mount. It was shameful to be a part of. We had even gone to the pub later and boasted how many of the little fuckers we killed.

'I hit four of them,' I boasted.

'Four... I shot at least ten,' Joe said.

'I killed forty-six of them,' Pete said. (The confusing fact was there were only about eighteen students playing the bloody game.)

Meanwhile, Rambo Roberts sat in the corner alone with a smirk on his face. I'm positive he had the decapitated head of one of the students in his rucksack.

Even today I still wonder what those students said about us when they got back to the student union bar. To me it was a real black day in the history of BS Consulting. To Rambo Roberts, I guess it was our greatest ever victory.

That was my first, but not my last, run-in with Nutcase Roberts. A few months later I supported him delivering several workshops in the Chicago area over a five-day period. It included us staying the weekend in the Windy City.

My first visit to America and I hated every minute of it. (Not America, the Rambo.) We turned out to be like chalk and cheese. Other than having the fresh blood of students on our hands, we had nothing in common at all.

Rambo had put the workshop together. As predicted, it was full of war references. Winston Churchill's name popped up throughout, so did Hitler's and I'm even sure Vald the Impaler came up as one of Roberts' role models.

For some bizarre reason he included one of his very own exercises in the session. He wanted me to run it. The whole thing didn't make sense. One thing I learnt from my terrible experience working with The Glass Is Always Half Full partner was to never stand up in front of people if I didn't believe in what I was talking about. So while Rambo told the audience how great Churchill was in wartime, but how bad he was in peacetime, I decided to make some adjustments to improve the exercise.

During coffee break I explained to Rambo what I had

done and, more importantly, why I had done it. He wasn't listening.

'You do it as it is,' he barked.

'Look... it's better like...'

'No,' he yelled, 'do it as it is.'

'No.'

'Yes.'

'No.'

We ended up having a screaming match in the car park in the blazing Chicago sunshine. I stuck to my guns; I wasn't going through what I had gone through before in front of a room full of strangers. I told him to stick his exercise up his paintballing, cheating arse and stormed off. He ended up running the exercise alone.

That night we went out for a meal. The frostiest hour and a half of my life. But my misery had only just started.

On the Saturday night we booked into a hotel on the main strip in Chicago city centre. A great hotel situated right in the heart of the action. I fancied going to a Blues club. Not surprisingly, Rambo wasn't into music or the arts. Knowing him, he probably wanted to go to a gun club and shoot boy scouts. He decided we should go to Hooters to sample the chicken wings and ogle young girls' tits.

I'd never been to Hooters before. The food wasn't bad and the girls were quite easy on the eye. But it still wasn't my idea of an ideal Saturday in Chicago. I could have chicken wings and see girls' tits (outside the bra) on a rainy Monday afternoon in Wetherspoon's in Merthyr. I wanted some American culture, not this.

Rambo sat there, like some old pervert with his tongue and his true colours hanging out. When we left I again mentioned going to a Blues club.

'No, let's go shopping.'

Being the younger, and less experienced traveller, I felt obliged to go along with him. I'm not sure why.

After about forty minutes I made my mind up. I was going

to do a runner. I had grown up in Merthyr running away from Indians and taxis, so escaping from Rambo Roberts shouldn't be hard to do. In one of the big department stores, I made my move. While he was looking at camouflaged jackets (honest to God) I ducked down among a rack of jeans and waited. I would have shot the twat with a gun but I know he would have said I missed him. I waited for him to go up the escalator to the next floor before I made a dash for it. I ran out of the store.

I headed as far away up the strip as I could. I settled down in an Irish bar and got smashed. All my built-up aggression slowly released with every pint of Guinness I drank. I had a cracking time talking to the locals. Mostly all one hundred per cent plastic, Irish Yanks, except for one guy. He had scraggy hair, a fisherman's jumper, a thick Belfast accent and killer eyes. Proper IRA. He scared the shit out of me.

Around midnight I strolled back to my hotel, worse for wear.

Next morning I played dumb when I met Rambo at breakfast. To be honest, I think he was glad we had lost each other. He probably went back to Hooters to tell all the girls about how he had single-handedly wiped out a squadron of commie students in the war.

For the rest of the trip small talk between us was painful. Yet again, I couldn't wait to get home.

He got sacked a few weeks later after several clients complained about his behaviour during a workshop. Last I heard Rambo Roberts lived in a tree, and dressed in bearskin with a bow and arrow. The best place for him I think.

11

Sex, Drugs and Chicken Parms

WHAT IS IT about the north-east which brings out the worst, or the best, in people? Is it something in the water up there which turns everyone into sex-starved, party zombies? The place seemed to be a magnet for every kind of sex, drugs and chicken parm imaginable.

I got to work for a few months in the shadow of the impressive Angel of the North delivering NVQs in Business Improvements. The objective was to train up groups of individuals from several companies to become experts in Continuous Improvement while achieving a recognised nationwide qualification. It proved to be a very successful programme and a good money-making machine for our business, and at least the natives in that part of the world understood my bloody accent.

The madness started on my very first flight from Cardiff to Newcastle to kick off the programme. Like most men, and some women, I've dreamt of joining the Mile High Club. With any luck, I imagined sharing the experience with some sex-starved Virgin air hostess or perhaps Madonna in her prime. But, unlike most men, I did actually achieve it. Although it wasn't exactly the full McCoy, in my mind it still counts.

Next to me on the plane sat a girl who was, without doubt, sex on legs, or sex on a stick, or legs on a stick! This girl I guess was around twenty-three and oozed sex appeal. She was made to make your mouth water with her long black hair, curves where curves should be and eyes to die for. She wore a short tartan skirt and long beige boots. Of course I didn't take much notice of her! Sadly her handsome boyfriend sat the other side of her.

Just before we took off, she pulled out of her bag an Ann Summers catalogue. I tried not to look. Honestly, I tried hard to concentrate on trying not to look.

'How about these?' she giggled and pointed at a photo of a girl in crotch-less panties.

Her boyfriend grinned.

I gulped.

She whispered something in his ear. I didn't know what it was but I assumed it wasn't about Sunday school and chocolate muffins.

When the plane took off, so did she. She knew exactly what she was doing. 'Which one of these should I buy?' She motioned to the page littered with sexy dressing up uniforms.

'The policewoman one... the policewoman one,' I nearly yelled out.

As if she had read my dirty mind, she whispered, 'Mmmmmm... I like the policewoman one... very sexy.' She rubbed his leg.

Maybe I was sitting by the wheel on the plane, but I suddenly had a boner. Is that a truncheon in your pants or are you just pleased to see me? I lowered the plastic tray thing to try and hide it. I'm sure she saw it. She whispered into his ear. He smiled. I wanted her to whisper into my ear. I know that's a terrible thing to say.

The place stunk of sex, or it may have been the EasyJet's tuna sandwiches, I'm not sure. What I did know was she had the both of us where she wanted us. Or in my mind she did. She probably thought I was an old, boring, dirty fucker with a hard-on.

I needed to do something. I'm not too ashamed to say I squeezed past her and headed gingerly to the toilet. Once in there I bashed a tune out on my organ like it's never been bashed before. It was all over in about a minute. I tried not to make any sound and I made sure I washed all the evidence away. I didn't want a *There's Something about Mary* hair sticking-up scene when I got back to my seat.

The devil's own sex toy looked me up and down and grinned when I got back. I must have been bright red, but thankfully my penis fell fast asleep, well for about twenty minutes.

The first few months I found myself stationed in the wonderful seaside town of Redcar. A mini-Blackpool but a hundred times more rundown. One night, I decided to go alone to the cinema on the promenade to see the newly-released film, *Shaun of the Dead*. The cinema was a big, old-fashioned, listed white building. It must have looked great in its heyday. Now, it badly needed a facelift and a lick of paint.

When I got to my seat I noticed I was the only one in there. It was freezing cold and the place smelt of damp and greasy chips. I was just about to ask for my money back when an old guy sauntered up to me. 'Are you cold son?' he asked.

I nodded.

He returned holding a three-bar electric fire and plugged it in. I was stoked. I sat there eating a Curly Wurly, with my toes lovely and warm, while watching Simon Pegg save Britain from zombies. In the end, it was so hot I took off my coat, scarf, gloves and bobble hat.

I stayed in a boarding house with a shared bathroom. One Thursday night I jumped out of the bath to get ready for dinner. Don't worry I didn't get caught jacking off in a plastic cup again. With a towel wrapped around me, I remembered I needed to send an important email to a possible new client. While waiting to get an Internet connection, for some stupid reason, I unplugged the mains cable from my computer and put it in my mouth. It was live.

BANG!

The electric shock knocked me clean off my chair. I lay there on the floor, legs in the air, my tackle hanging out. After several minutes I clambered to my feet. I looked in the mirror. My eyes bulged in my head and my hair stuck up like one of the Jedward twins. I wasn't sure if I was lucky to be alive, or the dullest person in the village. Probably both. I never did that again, and I never told anyone about it either. Well, not until now.

Another disadvantage of having no bathroom in my room meant the small sink in the corner became the centre of my world. Well, for most things anyway. Nine times out of ten, if I needed a pee, I simply flopped my old boy in the sink, ran the tap and let nature take its course.

Disgusting, I know. But, it saved a long hike to the cold bathroom on the next floor.

I got so blasé about doing this, I used to brush my teeth at the same time. Who said a man can't multi-task? As the days turned into weeks, it became a way of life for me. My daily and nightly routines saw me brushing my teeth while simultaneously relieving myself. I must admit there were many mornings while, slightly hungover, I peed over my toothbrush by mistake and was too slow to stop myself putting it into my mouth. (Now that is disgusting.)

My unusual peeing habit did become an issue on weekends when I went home. One Sunday morning my wife entered our en-suite and screamed. 'What the fuck are you doing?'

'What?' I innocently stood there, penis dangling in the sink, with a mouth full of Colgate toothpaste.

Before I could explain, she hit me with the toilet brush. Like a dog, or a baby, I had to get toilet trained all over again.

The group I was training were a mix of men and women in their twenties or early thirties. All of them party animals. I think every one of them said that 'socialising' (aka getting pissed) was their main hobby. I'm not saying they were as bad as the cast from *Geordie Shore*, but they weren't far off.

During my first week I showed the class a DVD about a really cool business selling fish in a Seattle outdoor market. The powerful but fun message was all about getting the right mix of individuals in the business to create a good team and then getting the team to focus on all aspects of delighting the customer.

When the DVD finished, I switched the light back on in

the room. Everyone sat there buzzing about the programme except for one. Millie looked like she would be more at home chained to a fence at a military nuclear plant in Greenham Common with the rest of the mothers-of-the-earth types than in a classroom. She wore Doc Martens, had a pierced nose and short, unkempt hair and wore the drabbest clothes ever invented. She turned out to be everything I expected from my first impression of her. A veggie, a vegan, a Klingon, an anti-this and anti-that. I don't think men were her favourite species either.

It was obvious by her sour puss that she wasn't happy by what she had seen.

She piped up. 'Some poor fish died during the making of that video.'

'What?'

'Fish were killed because of that nonsense.' Her face was the colour of the sun.

'Millie,' I laughed, 'It's a fish market... they sell fish. I think, but I could be wrong here, that most of the time the fish are dead by the time they get there.'

Some people in the room laughed. She didn't. She stood up and stared at me. She wasn't tall, but very stocky. For one terrible moment I thought she was going to race across the room and slam-dunk me to the floor, and then sit on me. I clutched my fists, just in case. I wasn't sure if I should leg it, or stand my ground and hit her as she bounded towards me. Maybe I could move out of the way and hope she'd fall out of the window on the pavement below. Thankfully, she turned and stormed out of the door. I never saw her again. Thank God.

One wild girl kept asking me and the team to go for a few beers to her local which wasn't far from the factory. One Thursday, after a tough week, we went along. The pub would have put the Jockey on the TV programme *Shameless* to shame. At 4.30 in the afternoon the place was bouncing. The smell of Bob Hope and aggression wafted through the air. All the men had shaved heads and tattoos from head to toe. All the women wore miniskirts which looked like they belonged to their much younger and thinner daughters.

Everything stopped when we walked in. One of our team wore a tie. The pub regulars thought we were coppers. The girl shouted out, 'They're OK, they're with me.' He removed his tie quickly.

Music blared, intense card games played out on various tables. And for big money too. One guy had two lurchers under his table. The only thing missing was a horse in the corner and gun holsters on the bar staff.

As the night got rowdier, and we got drunker, the girl who had taken us there told us her confession. 'I used to be a sex addict,' she enlightened us, 'I was into all the S&M clubs and swingers and stuff.'

'Used to be a sex addict?' one of the boys commented.

'Yeah,' she replied, her face looked quite sad, 'I was addicted. I even had my clit pierced.' I physically shivered at the thought, but not as much as I shivered when she told us the next part. 'Yeah it was great. It would make me cum just by walking across the shop floor.' I pictured her doing a *When Harry Met Sally* orgasm scream in between the stillages of stock in the stores. She added, 'One afternoon me and my boyfriend were having sex when he accidentally pulled the stud out. It ripped half my clit out with it. Now I've got no feeling at all.'

Even the lurchers winced. I felt sick.

Luckily, we were saved from any more gruesome details when a man came up to our table and asked if we wanted to buy half a sheep.

'The top half or the bottom half?' I joked.

He glared at me. 'Are you trying to be fucking funny, mate?'

I didn't want to say I was, and it was quite a witty response. I shook my head. He walked away. It was that type of place.

I must admit I turned into something of a party animal after that. Night after night we just needed any excuse for the group to meet up and sink a few.

It's bonfire night... let's go out tonight!
It's December the 3rd... let's go out tonight!
I just saw a black cat squashed flat in the middle of the road
– we must go out tonight or it will be bad luck!

I had a great laugh but it was hard work. I was there for more or less three months straight. Most nights I didn't get to bed until two in the morning. Very unprofessional of me, I know, but good fun. Next morning, I would be up at eight to set the room up for the lessons at nine. By the time I got home on a Friday I felt, and looked, like I had been on a rugby tour. I slept most of the weekend, and then travelled back up on the Sunday night.

I needed at least one week off the piss or I would have ended up booking into rehab. Making excuses after each session, I locked myself away in my hotel. My aim was no drinking, only eating healthy grub all week and plenty of sleep.

Monday night I sat alone in the little restaurant scanning the menu.

'Have you tasted our speciality?' the plump waitress asked.

'What's that?'

She dropped a spoon on the floor with a clank. 'Chicken parm... it's the best in the entire world.'

'Oh!'

An old woman on the next table chipped in, 'You must try our chicken parms, love... they're lovely... they're gorgeous.'

Everyone in the restaurant looked at me and smiled. No one moved as I scanned the menu. 'OK... I'll give it a try.'

'Good choice, sir,' the waitress replied. 'Our chicken parms are really the best in the world.' She licked her lips, as if there was something seriously wrong with her.

I didn't want to burst her bubble by saying the rest of the world hadn't fucking heard of it. I couldn't wait to see what it was. When it arrived, it came with a fanfare and a golden carriage. The chef walked along side it with all his family. OK, I made that up. The waitress carried it on a huge tray with a big slice of homemade bread. Basically, it was a giant turkey burger, the size of a car tyre, with enough cheese on the top to give a well-trained athlete a heart attack just by running past it.

'Fuck goes my eating healthy to start with,' I thought.

I took my first bite at around 8.15 p.m. on that Monday night. I was still eating it at 10.35 p.m. the following bloody Wednesday. It was tasty mind. Years later, I went to Ohio, and their speciality was also chicken parm. And believe it, or not, the Yanks also boasted their chicken parm was the best in the world. The only difference I could tell was the American version was the size of two car tyres, swimming in a wheelbarrow of cheese.

With chicken parm finally finished I was just about to go to bed, when a girl sitting at the next table in the small hotel bar shouted across, 'Where you from, butt?' in a thick Welsh accent.

'Merthyr Tydfil.'

'Fucking hell girls... he's from Merthyr,' she yelled to her mates. 'We're from Ebbw Vale, butt... Up here doing some shopping.'

That was it. Any thoughts of me going to bed early and not drinking disappeared. Six hours later we were still sat in the bar, drinking cider and playing games to drink more cider. Next morning I honestly couldn't see, or talk, or hear properly. White as a ghost, I swayed at the front of the classroom. My head wouldn't function. I looked at the group sitting in front of me waiting for me to do something. If it hadn't been raining I would have taken them for a walk in the nearby forest. Hopefully, we would have come across the cottage owned by The Three Bears and I could have climbed into bed and gone to sleep.

I concentrated hard just to be able to talk. Mid-flow and without prior warning, I accidently sneezed. A blob of snot landed on the desk. The disgust on the faces of the audience was evident as they stared at me. I looked down. The snot looked like an embryo floating about under a microscope. I tried to slyly flick it off, which only made it spread out even more. One girl heaved.

'Sorry,' I lied, 'I've got a terrible cold.'

Someone handed me some soluble tablets. Without thinking, I popped them into my mouth and then gulped down some water. Suddenly, my mouth just exploded. Foam escaped out of the sides, down my chin and all over my shirt. I looked like a rabid dog running around the room.

I told everyone I felt too ill to continue and sent them home. I went back to my hotel and went straight to bed.

After my drunken insane sessions in Redcar, I moved a few miles down the road to work at a large service company. I imagined the office environment to be less full in my face and a lot more subdued.

Wrong!

Within ten minutes of me setting my stuff up, one of the office guys ambled up to me and quietly muttered. 'Have you seen It yet?'

'It... what do you mean, It?'

He grinned. 'So you haven't seen It.'

'What are you talking about? It what?'

He just laughed and walked away. I shrugged and continued drawing up the day's agenda on the flip chart. About ten minutes later someone, or something, stood in front of me, blocking out the light.

'Do you want a cup of tea?' a deep voice asked.

I looked up. It was then I realised what It was. It, referred to by the guy not me, was a massive six-foot two-inch, black transvestite called Shamu (like the Disney whale character, but only much fuckin' bigger). The trannie wore a smart, purple jacket with matching pencil skirt. Thick red lipstick, red blusher and black fishnet stockings. I couldn't help but stare at It, sorry he (or she). I didn't know.

'Hum... What?' I eventually said.

'Do you want a cup of tea?' It licked its lips.

For a few seconds I was too shocked to answer. I nodded my head. 'Just with milk, please.'

'Thought so,' It said, 'you're sweet enough.' Shamu winked at me then waddled away like Jessica Rabbit walking down the catwalk in a Miss Rabbit contest.

I looked about. The other guys in the office sat about pissing themselves laughing.

'It's got a real hard spot for you,' one shouted across the room.

I didn't know if I had been set up or what? But Shamu was real. For the rest of my time there, It kept popping up and making me tea and offering me biscuits. It even made me a cheese sandwich. I didn't eat it and kept out of It's way as much as I could.

During the second week of the course the group had got to know each other, and me, a little better. Another consultant, Pete, had joined me to carry out a section of the training. We introduced a great little ice breaker where each member told the rest of the group three things about themselves. Two of the facts had to be real and the other one false.

I started the ball rolling with my usual three:

I used to play drums in a punk rock band.

I have a three-legged dog called Lucky.

I won a Welsh international rugby cap.

You get the picture. (If you want to know which is true and false for me go to the end of the book.)

The ice breaker started off well. Very light-hearted with lots of laughter floating about. Up next came a slightly chubby and serious-looking girl. Maybe spending five years serving in the army had made her like that – serious, not chubby.

Unlike the others, she stood up as she read out her three facts. They went like this:

I once met Kylie Minogue.

I once got drunk with footballer Micky Quinn.

I got thrown out of the army for sleeping with the general's daughter.

Everyone laughed when she finished.

The girl didn't.

'All right group,' I said, 'which one is false.'

'You have never met Kylie Minogue,' someone said.

'I have,' she replied, 'I met her when she played in Newcastle. I went backstage. She was wonderful.' The girl even managed a smile.

Everyone seemed suitably impressed.

'OK,' one of the boys chipped in, 'you have never got drunk with the legend that is Micky Quinn.'

From that moment on, everything changed. Everything in the room moved in slow motion. The chubby girl stared at the boy. 'I have. He used to drink in my local when I was growing up.'

'Oh,' the boy said.

'Oh.' I looked across at Pete. He shrugged his shoulders, and rolled his eyes.

'Oh,' said everyone else.

The girl stood there, staring at everyone in turn. The rest of the class sat in shock, their minds ticking over. The image in my head was too unprintable for this book.

'Right,' I clapped my hands, 'let's have a coffee break.'

Pete and I sat in silence while everyone went to the canteen.

'Did she just...?' I didn't want to say it.

'I think she did,' he replied.

I couldn't understand it. Surely if someone was going to step out of the closet, there must have been better ways and places to do it? Maybe she could have written a book? Or leaked it to the local newspaper? Or ideally, turn up for work in a checked shirt, Bill Stunt jeans and Doc Martens, for fuck sake. Maybe she didn't think it was a big deal?

When the group came back I ploughed straight into another exercise, trying my best not to mention lesbians, strap-on dildos and prawn sandwiches. I nearly cracked several times while talking about culture change. There was a little awkwardness for a short while but by the next morning everything continued as normal.

During those couple of weeks I stayed in a hotel just outside the town of Yarm. For some strange reason, on a Tuesday night the small town had more nightlife than any town or city had on most weekends. I'd been told it all started when gangs of loose women went on the pull looking for rich footballers playing for one of the big Premier clubs up in that neck of the woods. Apparently, lots of the superstars lived around the town and Tuesday was their night off. Not sure if it was true, or not, but whatever the reason the place was bloody rammed.

I often went in there to have something to eat and people-watch the natives. It was unbelievable. I saw one Middlesbrough football star pull a wedge of fifty-pound notes out of his pocket and order about thirty bottles of champagne. Girls hung off him like shit on a stick. The jammy, lucky, wealthy bastard.

I stayed in a Travelodge hotel very close by. Each time I stayed, they put me in the same room. Room 206. Every Tuesday night when I got back to my room there was always some kind of depraved, sexual orgy taking place in the room next door. Sweaty bodies, long pointy tongues, dark crevices and penis-shaped devices got explored with abandon. OK, I wasn't sure about the details, but that was the scene playing out in my mind while I listened.

A woman screamed out as if she was being murdered with a meat cleaver. A man moaned and groaned like he was moving a large piano upstairs by himself. I lay in bed listening to this for hours and hours.

To make matters worse, on my ceiling there were strange marks, which I convinced myself were whip marks. I routinely assumed a midget had been bouncing on my bed whipping someone. I instantly thought of the little interpreter from the paper cup business. I cursed my imagination at times. I cursed Mister Miyagj for not speaking English.

On Wednesday morning, I told some of the people in my workshop about my eventful night. They didn't believe me. I even took photos of my whip-marked ceiling to show them the next day. They still didn't believe me.

'But why a midget?' a woman asked me.

I drew it up on the flip chart. I showed her that a normal-sized man couldn't stand on a normal-sized bed and use a normal-sized whip. So it had to be a midget. It didn't occur to me until just now it could have been a normal-sized man not bouncing on the bed, but standing on the floor instead. Or a normal-sized man bouncing on the bed with a midget-sized whip!

I think the group thought I was mental. To be truthful, after living up there for months, I think I was.

However, every Tuesday night the orgy next door took place. It was never any other night. Never a Monday, or a Wednesday, or a Thursday. It made me wonder:

Who were the couple?

Were they having some fabulous, illicit affair?

Was she a prostitute?

Was he a prostitute? (Anything went in Yarm, I had been informed.)

Was he fat? Was she fat?

Did he shop at Top Shop? I didn't know why I thought of that. I think because there was an advert for Top Shop on when I listened one night.

Once, their love-making turned me on so much I nearly knocked on the door and ask could I join in, or at least, watch? Maybe I would ask the man if I could help him to move the piano? Would they understand what I meant and let me in? What if he was really trying to move a piano, and she was lying on the bed with a meat cleaver in her head? Would I still help him move it? I doubted it.

However, I chickened out at the last minute. I went back to my room and I lay on the bed, staring at the whip marks. I wondered what they did after the final screams and moans died down. I wondered what the midget with the whip was doing now. Then, one Tuesday night, I heard nothing. No sound, no love making, no piano moving. I wondered what had happened. Had they moved rooms? Had they stopped having an affair? Had he run out of money and couldn't afford a hooker anymore? Had he died from eating too many French fries?

Whatever the reason I missed them. They had become part of my Tuesday night ritual. I felt betrayed and let down. They could have left me a note. Just pushed it under the door to tell me they were off. But they left me with nothing. How selfish were they?

Life was never the same. Pretty soon after that I was back on the road to nowhere yet again.

12

Joining the Occult

I WAS CHUFFED when asked if I wanted to become a partner in the business. Out of the blue, the partners asked five of us if we would like to go all the way and take a walk on the wild side. At first, I wasn't sure if I should accept the offer or not. I hadn't had much luck down the years when joining various clubs.

The cubs – I lasted three weeks after some fat boy gave me a vicious snakebite on my arm and made me cry.

The scouts – I lasted a week longer. But football was much more important than getting a purple badge for helping old people carry their shopping bags across the road.

Even when I joined the secret world of the masons, I only stuck it for one night. To be honest, it really wasn't my cup of tea from the start. Plus, on the night of my grand induction, the top, top Mason secretly told me how he and his wife had been abducted by aliens the week before. I thought he meant he'd been mugged by illegal aliens.

'No,' he looked me in the eyes, 'the real space creatures. They took us up in their spaceship.'

I unrolled my trouser leg, got my coat and left, never to return.

So, with my past disasters fresh in my memory, I really wasn't sure if I was cut out to become a partner of anything. I didn't want to join something unless my heart was really in it. Also, many people believed, me included, that it would be the beginning of the end for **BS Consulting**. Some of the consultants who had worked for the business for longer than me, like Tom, and who hadn't been asked, felt betrayed. I didn't blame them. I would have been the same if the shoe had been on the other foot.

It caused a massive rift. There was no longer just an 'us (the consultants) and them (the partners)' divide. That had always existed, no matter how hard The Glass Is Always Half Full partner tried to convince everyone it didn't. Overnight it had now grown bigger, with a new 'us (the consultants) and them (the partners), and them (the new partners)' divide.

However, after considering my other options, rather selfishly, I agreed to step over the line. No one could blame me, really.

So, from being a simple, self-employed consultant working for the business, I became a self-employed partner working for the same business. Deep-down and despite the resentment from others, I was pleased. I think the partners could see something in the five of us to help take the business forward.

Once I signed my soul away to the devil (or away to The Master, 5-Star Gimp, The Prof and The Glass Is Always Half Full partner, to be more precise), I began to wonder if I should start to act differently. Act more like a partner since I was now part of their world. Should I try to look more intelligent? Maybe smoke a pipe or wear a jacket with arm patches?

At my first ever partners' meetings, like David Attenborough studying the mating behaviour of the male gorillas, I scrutinised the partners very closely. They all appeared extremely confident as they put their points across. Their voices boomed into every corner of the room. They never seemed to let their consultant crown slip. And they did love the sound of their own voices. No matter how trivial the point, they all had to say something. Each one of them deemed it necessary to add something extra on to whatever someone else had said.

It all seemed like a game to me. In the first meeting, The Glass Is Always Full partner said, 'I think we should open an office in Ireland.'

'Yes… great idea. I think we should open an office in Ireland and call it the Irish Office,' added one of the new partners.

I thought, 'You cocky bastard. You've only been a partner for two bloody minutes and you are already opening offices in Ireland.' I had a lot to learn.

'Brilliant,' the fashion-conscious partner added, 'I definitely think we should open an office in Ireland, and call it the Irish Office, and maybe we can wear green polo shirts with our name on them.'

'I could then be known as The Prof of Ireland,' the Prof said.

'And if you are The Prof of Ireland, I can be The Sales Director of Ireland. I'll go and phone my wife now,' The Glass Is Always Half full partner piped up.

The meeting went on, and on, and on, and on. I wanted to be a partner but I wasn't sure if I could live in this world. The following meeting started off the same, more or less.

The Glass Is Always Full partner said, 'Let's open an office in Sweden.'

'Sweden? What about Ireland?' I jumped in.

'Never mind Ireland… full of leprechauns and bombers… Sweden is brilliant, and we could call it the Swedish Office.'

'Brilliant. And in the Swedish Office we could have all Ikea furniture…' again one of the new partners said.

'Shit,' I thought, 'I'm getting left behind here!'

'Yes… And I could be The Prof of Sweden,' muttered The Prof.

'And if you are The Prof, I could be The Sales Director of Sweden. I'll go and tell my wife; she loves Ikea and Abba.'

And the whole thing started over again, like cars on the Indie 500 track. Going around and around, and to be honest, not getting anywhere. I knew if I was going to survive I needed to be more confident and definitely learn to enjoy, or just accept, the experience and all the bullshit. But I found it hard.

I rushed to the library to see if there were any books to help me. I found an entire section on consultants, cowboys and bullshitters. In fact many of the books in there had been written by The Prof himself. To be honest they bored the pants off me within the first five pages. They live in my garage now with all my DIY tools!

But however much reading I didn't do, I still nearly became the shortest ever partner in the history of people becoming partners. Not even two weeks after signing up, as I almost lost my marbles and my job.

*

Several times while doing my job I've wanted to punch someone really hard. On more than one occasion, it was not just punching. I wanted to kick, stamp and drive over certain individuals with a steamroller just to ensure I didn't have to see them again.

I'd just finished running a workshop in Bristol, when I had a phone call asking if I could run a quick workshop in a company in the Midlands the following morning. With my new partner's hat on, I agreed. The secretary from our office arranged the hotel for me.

'It's a decent three-star-ish hotel not far from the factory,' she informed me.

I got to the decent three-star-ish hotel around seven in the evening to find it was more like a no-star, run-down pub in a dead-end village. The place only had about twelve rooms but, at £20 a night without breakfast, at least it was cheap.

My room, located on the top floor, was decorated like something out of the Sixties. All oranges and browns with threadbare carpets and squeaky floorboards. It even had a lava lamp (which didn't work). I half-expected three flying birds on the wall, or a painting of a beautiful, dark-haired islander woman, like my Nan, and probably every other Nan in the UK, used have in her front room in those days.

But I was only staying for one night so what was the worst that could happen? I went down to have a bite to eat in the bar. What a big mistake. I ordered homemade pie and mash. When it came it looked like a horse with dysentery had shat it straight onto the plate, and then pissed weak gravy all over the top of it.

It tasted even worse than it looked. I played about with it on my plate for a bit before leaving it. My pint of Guinness looked like someone had put lumps of coal in lukewarm water and left it to stand on a radiator. I would have slyly tipped it in the pot of plastic flowers, but it would have probably killed them.

For all the time I was in the bar, I only saw two old guys come in. They had a pint, made a face and left. On the plus side at least it was quiet.

Next morning I got up early. The shower was so cold I gave it a miss. Instead, I shaved in the ice cold water in the small sink. When I put my empty shaving can in the swing bin I saw a pair of women's knickers staring back up at me. The tag hanging out informed me the owner was a size 16. What I wish I hadn't seen was the bloodied tampon stuck to its gusset.

I slammed the bin shut as if there was a two-headed dragon about to jump out of it.

Feeling quite sick, I got my stuff together and headed downstairs. Surprisingly, the reception area was completely deserted. There wasn't even a light on. I left my key on the desk and went to leave. But I couldn't. The main door was locked and bolted. I pulled and pushed for about five minutes. Nothing budged.

'Hello,' I shouted quietly at first. That soon changed after a few minutes to me bellowing at the top of my lungs.

I started to panic. Every man's dream must be to be locked in a pub. But not this pub, and not when I had a client to get to. I banged on the door. I thought about smashing the window. But they were covered on the outside with mesh.

I went back into my room to see if there was another way out. There wasn't.

I phoned Tom up. At first he called me a 'jammy bastard', and then he laughed his cock off and hung up.

Then I realised why breakfast hadn't been in the price. The fucking owners were nowhere to be seen. Probably still in bed somewhere else in the village.

Why didn't they tell me? Or leave me a key to get out?

I booted lumps out of the front door. I swore and sweated until my foot hurt. The door was reinforced with about ten inches of steel. I heard a noise outside. The postman, I thought. I screamed through the letterbox.

'Helllllllppppppppppppppppppppppppppppp me... rescue me... Ooooohhhhhhhhh.' I felt like a prat.

No one came.

Then I had a brainwave. I gathered up all the keys to the bedrooms from behind reception. In order, I went to each room to see if there was any chance of escape. After trying five consecutive rooms I finally found one with a fire exit door which wasn't padlocked!

I kicked the door open and raced down the old rusty stairs. But still my adventure wasn't over. At the back of the hotel I came face-to-face with a ten-foot wall with splinters of glass around the top. Fucking hell, I had managed to escape out of Colditz, and now I was faced with scaling the Berlin Wall.

Naturally, the door leading out into the road was locked as well. Using all my boy scout skills (all four weeks of them), I balanced several beer crates on top of one another. I inched my way to the top of the flimsy structure. It wobbled. I screamed. I fell off. I tried again. If YouTube had been going back then, and someone filmed it, I would have been an Internet sensation or viral clown. Eight times I tried before I managed to haul myself and my suitcase and computer bag over the Berlin Wall to safety.

I raced around the front of the pub and pissed through the letterbox. No, I didn't. But I should have fucking done it. I posted all the keys through instead. I wonder what the owners thought when they opened up that morning. But the way I felt

I couldn't care less. I sat in my car, angry and annoyed. Then I looked at the wall I had just scaled and actually burst out laughing.

Fifteen minutes later, I stood in a training room in a steel plant in Birmingham. A group of cynical, hard-arsed workers sat waiting for me to arrive. The director wanted to see if I could help the company to improve their delivery to their customers. Apparently, their on-time-delivery performance was less than twenty-five per cent.

I started the session by asking the group what they thought were the main issues with the day-to-day running of the business. Most of their responses were interesting and quite positive. But there's always one. The more experienced I got, the more I could just tell by someone's body language if they were going to be trouble. One guy, the head of planning, couldn't have looked more like trouble if he had turned up in steel toe-capped boots, skinhead braces and chanting anti-consultant football songs. He sat there arms folded, mouth turned down, rolling his eyes.

I asked him what he thought.

'Nothing,' he said. 'We're doing OK.'

'Doing OK?' I chipped back, 'Your delivery performance is terrible. Probably the worst I've ever seen.' Sometimes in my job I had to be cruel to be kind.

'It's not that bad,' he fired back.

'Not bad...! You're only shipping out twenty-five per cent of your orders on time. Imagine going to a restaurant and only the chips came out on time.'

'Our customers don't mind.'

I ignored him, and wrote down the suggestions from the others. Every time someone said something, the planning guy muttered loudly and shook his head. After forty minutes I'd had enough. No. After about five minutes I'd had enough, I was just being polite. I thought he may suddenly see the light or a coil of steel would fall on his thick, stubborn head. Sadly, neither happened.

'OK... how can you improve?' I threw an open question out to the team.

The planning guy piped up first. 'We should tell the customer to stop giving us unrealistic demands.'

'Are you fucking serious?' I know I shouldn't have sworn but I did. 'They are the customer. They can give you whatever demands they want.'

'No, they can't.'

'Yes, they can.'

'Oh no they can't.'

'Oh yes they can.'

It turned into a bad scene from a poor pantomime. There were twelve people in the room, but in my eyes there were just two. Me and the donkey in a two-way Mexican stand-off. I wasn't backing down.

He carried on down his dead-end route. I carried on trying to drive us back the other way. We got nowhere fast.

I snapped. 'OK... outside,' I yelled. Everyone looked at me. 'No... I don't mean outside, outside. I mean let's have a look around this wonderful plant of yours.' To be honest a big part of me wanted to take him outside and kick the shit out of him, and get the steamroller.

We walked around the plant. Even when I pointed stuff out to him, he got so defensive. I wasn't doing it for personal gain or satisfaction. I had a job to do and often that meant exposing the worst flaws in the way organisations operated. It felt like Germany and Mathias all over again.

The more we walked, the more we argued. I wanted to wring his neck. Back in the room, we had a stand-up screaming match.

'What do you know anyway?' he grinned. 'You are probably a failed production manager, I bet.'

I stepped towards him. He stepped back, nearly falling over a table. I came up, nose-to-nose.

'And you are definitely a failed fucking planner.'

In the end someone stepped in between us.

I stormed to the head honcho's office. Taking a leaf out of Tom's book, I told him I was off and he should call me back if the planning guy was demoted, sacked or killed in some evil way. I know I shouldn't have reacted like I did. But I could have made a big difference to the business. I was passionate about what I did. I was there to help them, not have a fist-fight in the fucking car park with some idiot.

The manager complained to The Master about my behaviour. I had a dressing down from the main partners and was told to start acting like them!

Other than that little mishap, I was quite enjoying my new status as a junior partner. I even got to work with the great wizard known as The Prof. We travelled together to Belgium for a few days. I sat next to him in awe on the plane wondering what the hell I was going to say to him. We were from completely different worlds. He was from Mars, and I was a penis. I felt overpowered and intimidated by him, inferior in every way possible. Well except maybe playing football in the school yard in primary school.

To be fair, he did most of the talking. I sat and listened. I knew my place in the pecking order of consultant life. The Prof sat on top of the tree, I rolled about down in the mud with the worms and the slugs.

Not far outside Bruges, we went out for dinner with two directors from a global, car-part business. Within about fifteen minutes, I got the impression I was so insignificant to these guys they couldn't be bothered to talk to me at all. Not once did they involve me in their conversation. They rarely looked at me, neither did The Prof.

I'm the type of person that the longer I go without saying anything when I'm in a new group of people, I start to lose confidence, and the more likely it is I won't speak at all. And that's exactly what I did. I clammed up. I didn't say one word all night except 'I don't want any bread' to the waiter. And even he ignored me and brought me bread and put it on my plate.

To them I may as well have been the waiter, or the shoe-shine boy, or the bread.

They spent all night brown-nosing The Prof. He spent all night with his cords around his ankles letting them brown-nose him, while rabbiting on and on. It sounded like absolute bullshit to me. Good and realistic absolute bullshit, mind you, but bullshit all the same. The two ignorant idiots fell completely under his spell.

Just listening to him, I soon realised what The Prof was actually a professor in. It was in 'sounding very convincing even if, in my opinion, he seemed to be winging it!'. He was marvellous, absolutely brilliant. The two directors were no mugs. Probably on a six-figure salary plus benefits. But they were like soft putty in his crafty, old hands. He took them to the edge and let them dangle for a while. Then in good, old-fashioned consultant style, he informed them how he could save them and their business from certain death. They signed on the dotted line before the dessert tray appeared. And what's more, he charged the earth, and the moon, for the privilege. I've never seen anyone with bigger balls before. Not in the physical sense (although I've never seen his balls, so they may be the biggest balls I'd never seen).

I was bored to death. I sat through the longest three hours of my life. As my Nan once said about the new, modern, guitar-playing choir in her church, 'It was cruel.' I felt the same. I sat wishing two things would happen.

Either, I could fast-forward the evening a few hours, or even a few days and get it all over with. I wasn't enjoying it at all. I'd rather be in the crazy pub in Redcar getting tanked up with proper people and talking about clit rings. Or, better still, a young Al Pacino would walk out of the toilets holding a hand gun and shoot the three of them from point-blank range between the eyes. Then me and Al would go and get drunk and talk our own bullshit about films, music and important stuff like that.

13

Two-Tits from Amsterdam

FLYING INTO THE port of Amsterdam conjured up wicked images of Anne Frank, soft drugs and hard sex. And definitely not in that order.

I got invited to run a series of workshops just outside the infamous city of sin. Naturally, I did a little research on the net to find the places of real interest. I didn't know what to expect but I did know I was going to try my best to find out what all the fuss was about.

Unfortunately, I flew into Schiphol airport at 6 p.m. on a cold Monday night, to be greeted by the country's biggest snowfall in almost fifty years. After its third attempt, my plane just managed to land. The airport runway was car-jammed, or plane-jammed to be more precise. Nothing moved. All the incoming planes faced one direction, all the outgoing aircraft, the opposite way.

My plane didn't move an inch for six bloody hours. Six hours of sitting there, cold and hungry. The only thing they offered us were the world-famous KLM cheese sandwiches to munch on. During my entire plane travel throughout the world, the KLM cheese sandwich still holds a special little place in my heart, along with salty pretzels and meatballs. The sandwiches are so bad, the first time I sampled it, I thought it was a joke. If I was the king I'd make the KML management eat them non-stop on a flight, just so they could find out how disgusting they are.

That night, the businessmen on the flight were up in arms. They moaned and groaned and blamed everyone for the mess we were in. Some shouted and raised their voices at the air stewardesses like it was going to make a difference. OK, even I blamed them for their slow drinks service and not making us feel welcome when we got on, but it wasn't their bloody fault winter had arrived with a bang. Give them a break.

My time wasn't wasted though. Luckily for me I had just started writing a new book about a transvestite murderer called Derek. Don't ask me why, or how I thought of the idea. But it could have been a connection with the weird tranny from Redcar, or Teacher Bessie, my hometown TV who used to scare the life out of me when I was growing up!

Oblivious to anything around me, I sat scribbling away in a world of my own, writing nonsense. But I didn't care. It was my nonsense and much better than moaning or phoning everyone in my phone book to bore them with the details of how my plane was stuck. I felt quite relaxed, while everything around me went slowly mental. I'd turned a problem into an opportunity and written about four rough chapters.

Finally, just after midnight, we disembarked off the metal tube. By then I felt tired and hungry. I didn't know exactly where I was going to. I just had the name of the hotel written on a piece of paper.

As you can imagine, the terminal building was in complete chaos. People rushed about shouting and pushing each other. One guy raced passed me screaming that his computer had been nicked. He looked straight at me as though I could help. Gripping my own computer bag tightly, I headed outside for a taxi.

'Bollocks.' The queue for a taxi stretched way off into the distance. I felt like crying. It was definitely one of the few occasions when I felt like packing my job in and heading back home. It was freezing, even my thick coat proved useless against the cold, Dutch wind.

I trudged towards the back of the queue. Suddenly, a guy in a smart, dark overcoat and leather gloves appeared next to me.

'Do you need a lift, sir?' he politely asked.

'Yes,' I said without hesitation.

He motioned for me to follow him. I felt ten feet tall as I strolled past the line of losers waiting for a cab. I handed the guy the paper with my hotel address details on it. As we reached his black car, parked near the road, he grinned at me. The boot opened up. I placed my suitcase in, but held my computer bag in my arms.

Once inside the car, I slumped down in the back, exhausted. We headed off. I thought how bad it would be to still be waiting in the long queue, instead of sitting nice and warm in a strange car with a strange bloke I had never met before in my life. Then, reality hit me like a baseball bat across my head. What the fuck was I doing?

My mother's advice, to never take sweets, or get into cars with strange men, rang out in my ears. I know I was only seven at that time but it's something I should never have forgotten!

Was I being paranoid? Or just tired? He didn't look like a murderer. But neither did Dennis Nilsen or Harold Shipman – and look what they did.

The driver typed something into his sat nav. I breathed out and relaxed. Two miles outside the airport, we drove past another car with its bonnet up located in a dark, unlit spot by the side of the road.

'That's my friend,' the driver muttered, 'I must turn around.'

That's when terror took over from reality. He was Dennis Nilsen and Harold Shipman rolled into one person. I imagined Fred and Rose West ducked down in the back of the other car, waiting. I started shaking. I pictured myself getting beaten up and left for dead in a mud-filled ditch. Or worse still, imprisoned into a life of human trafficking. A white slave, getting bummed by sweaty businessmen in dark rooms, with no windows, one swinging light bulb and it all being filmed for hard-core, gay porn movies.

I instantly pictured my mates from the rugby club somehow getting a copy of it and all laughing at me on the fifty-eight-inch

TV in the lounge with surround sound, while eating faggots and penis, no sorry, peas.

How ironic?

The driver swung the car around. My heart pumped in my chest. I could hardly breathe.

'OK,' I thought, 'if I'm going down, I'm going down fighting.'

I slyly took my wallet out of my pocket and removed my own personal credit card. I hid it in my sock. The business credit card, computer and phone they could have.

'Oh no... my writing!' I wasn't going to let six hours' worth of quality, creative scribbling go to waste. I quietly ripped the pages out of my notepad and stuffed them in my shirt. (See, that's how committed I was to my art. I could have been on the verge of getting bummed senseless in less than five minutes then dumped in a river, yet I was more concerned with saving the imaginary life of Derek, the murdering transvestite.)

The driver pulled up behind the 'broken down' car. He jumped out. It was pitch black. I couldn't understand what they were talking about but I was sure I heard the words, 'Bum... squeal like a pig... and we could sell him in the sex market for a handsome profit, Mr West.'

They looked over at me. My driver walked back towards our car. I clenched my fists and my arse cheeks even tighter.

'Push,' he indicated.

What? Was that the first instruction into a long life of slavery?

I slowly got out. I wanted to show him photos of my kids and tell him how much they loved me. (I hoped.) Then I realised he really did want me to push... the car. I almost burst out laughing and hugged him.

I covered my hands with my jumper and pushed and slipped and pushed some more. We finally got it going. The other guy waved as he drove slowly away. I sat in the back of our car, smiling at my stupidity all the way to my hotel. It was three in the morning when I finally got there. The workshop started at

7 a.m. Fair play to the hotel owner, she was still up. She gave me a plate of food. It was only a ham and cheese salad, but it tasted like the best food I had ever had.

Dragging myself to the workshop on the first morning proved tough. Luckily, most of it was spent telling each other our best 'stuck in the snow' stories.

The rest of the trip went to plan, well, almost. One of the delegates, staying at the same hotel, went for a stroll on the beach one evening, and keeled over dead. Tragic. It put a real dampener on the rest of the week. Luckily, the next morning we spent ages telling each other the best 'delegate dropping dead in a workshop' story. And, as one of my colleagues later pointed out when I got back to the UK, 'Some people will do anything to get out of your workshop, Bunko.'

I dreaded the Secret Santa that Xmas!

With everything going on, I didn't have time or the nerve to venture into Amsterdam. I was gutted but I got the opportunity to go back a few weeks later. This time I was definitely going to see the sights if it was the last thing I did.

After the workshop on the first day, I made some excuse about not feeling well and went to my room. As soon as it got dark, like a soldier on a mission, I clambered out of the fire escape, hopped on a city train, and headed for the bright, red lights of Amsterdam.

Twenty minutes later, I wandered around the city clenching a small map, with a semi-lob on. Problem was I couldn't find what I was looking for. The image portrayed in the movies about Amsterdam is of a nice, friendly, chilled-out type of Bohemian city, full of hippy-types, and peace and love. It's not like that at all. It's a rough old joint. I needed my Merthyr wits about me, yet again.

As I walked, I noticed the shop window of an art gallery. I stopped to take a look. I couldn't believe it. They had real life-size models like the old Airfix planes, where you snapped off the pieces from a rectangular piece of plastic and glued them together. But these were not aeroplanes or submarines.

The concept was the same but this was really, weird, sick stuff. One was called Dead Raped Woman. Another was Little Boy Knocked Down By Tram. Who the hell would think of something like that? And why call it art? Imagine having friends around and unveiling Dead Raped Woman hanging in your dining room! I'm not sure who the sickest would be. The nutcase designing it or the odd-ball buying it!

It freaked me out a little. As I wandered down an alleyway, I suddenly stopped dead in my tracks. Facing me were row upon row of windows. Behind each glass, gorgeous girls, modelling the smallest outfit imaginable, smiled at me.

My tongue hung out of my mouth. I had never seen anything like it. Dead Raped Woman forgotten, I wandered about in a perverted trance. The smell of dope twirled around my nostrils. A large sign for a live sex show caught my attention.

'Oh, when in Rome,' I muttered.

I sat in the front row (not on purpose... honest) in a cramped room which held about fifty people. A series of lovely-looking girls appeared one by one on the stage. Each one performed a different, mind-boggling act. It ranged from stretching their legs over their head, to firing ping pong balls, Sticky Vicky from Benidorm style, from their nether regions. One guy next to me actually caught one... in his mouth. The dirty bastard!

For the main attraction, a girl and a thick-set black guy took centre stage. Bloody hells bells, the guy made John Holmes look like Wee Willie Winkie. *(Note to readers: never take wife or girlfriend to see show unless you also can make John Holmes look like Wee Willie Winkie.)*

During the interval, I glanced around. Nearly everyone crammed into the room were Chinese. Row upon row of them. They all sat there staring at the stage while passing around sweets. I think they were sherbet lemons. Bizarre, but bloody hilarious

Then I saw him. A white, English face stared directly at me.

'Fuck I know him,' I thought. Trust my luck. He was one of

the delegates from my class. A guy in his early thirties, with a red scarf tied around his neck. I wondered if I could hide. Too late, he waved at me. He came over. After a few awkward moments, we both ended up laughing and promising not to tell the others.

We decided not to stay for the second half of old big cock's show, the big show-off. Instead we found a bar and had a few drinks.

'Fancy going to a brown café?' he asked. I'm glad he did, because the smell of dope smelt so tempting.

I've never smoked cigarettes in my life, not even a puff. However, I'm not ashamed to admit that I have sampled the odd spliff, and the odd soft drug, when growing up. I don't believe there's anything wrong with it, as long as it's done in moderation and then left alone.

Not being a smoker, the nicotine normally does me in before the dope. I'm one of those 'two puffs then pass it on' kind of dope smoker. I did smoke a joint all by myself once (after watching the film *American Beauty*). I ended up going lime green and spewing for four hours.

So, me and my new secret mate went in search of paradise. We brought two pre-rolled joints in the brown café and settled down in the corner. A scruffily dressed man next to us, who looked like he lived under a bridge or he should have lived under a bridge, shook his head at our stash.

'That stuff is shite. Try one of these.' He reached inside his smelly coat and handed me one of his homemade spliffs.

Of course, it would have been impolite not to accept his gift. I took a few drags before passing it around.

Wow! I could feel the difference straight away. Like chalk and high quality Colombian cheese. He rolled another one. He kind of smirked as he handed it to me. I puffed away.

The full force of it hit me. Like a nuclear explosion right between the eyes. The room stopped moving, completely. There was no sound, no nothing. I could hear my heart beating. Then my world spun around and around like I was stuck on a waltzer in the fairground. It got faster and faster. Paranoid thoughts replaced any normal ones left in my head. I imagined the joint-offering tramp, who lived under a bridge or should have lived under a bridge, was out to kill us. Well, not us, me. Then I believed the guy from my class was in cahoots with him. Both out to get me and dump me in the canal, but of course, bum me first.

I don't remember leaving. I do remember being out in the street with people rushing past me.

The guy from the class stood directly in front of my face. 'What's wrong?' his voice drilled into my brain.

'Quick, the tramp guy is going to kill us,' I muttered, 'He can't bum me... I'm a consultant.' The guy looked at me oddly. I took off up a side street like an ostrich in platform boots. I stopped. I felt faint. People whizzed past. He took my arm and sat me down on a bench.

Fifteen minutes later, the mist clouding my brain began to clear. I began to feel normal-ish again. I'm not sure if Tramp Man had spiked me or if it was just some super, strong stuff. But I learnt a lesson. Never take joints off trampy-looking blokes in black overcoats in brown cafés in Amsterdam and always take sherbet lemons to strip shows.

So I had been, seen, but definitely not conquered, the infamous Amsterdam. That was enough of the high-rolling, drug-taking life for me. The rest of the week I sat in my hotel eating sweet bread (by mistake) and drinking small glasses of strong lager and listening to the barman telling me all about where asparagus came from.

*

I got to hate Amsterdam and especially Schiphol airport with a passion. Nearly every time I used the airport I got delayed or my baggage ended up in a tin hut in India while I travelled to Portugal. On the plus side, there was a café upstairs in the terminal building which made the most wonderful meatballs ever. I would salivate as soon as I went through passport control on my way back.

Late that Friday night, I sat in the business lounge chilling out waiting to go home. Meatballs already eaten, I sat back to do a spot of reading. It was about 9 p.m. I had been working in a company organising their cold store. It had gone rather well. Especially since the giant of a storeman who, at the start of the week, I feared was going to strangle and then eat me, actually thought I was a genius by the time I left. And all I had done was tidy up!

I relaxed in the lounge with a glass of wine and a copy of *NME*. I glanced around at the rest of the lost souls who should have been with their loved ones at that time of night. Ninety-nine point nine per cent of the people in the lounge were men, nearly all businessmen. All kitted out in shirt, ties, suits and polished brogues. Most of them still on their computers, or still discussing work on their phones. I could hear loud conversations concerning logistics and culture and all kinds of other boring stuff.

I wondered if these guys were so bad at their job that they couldn't let it go for one minute. Was the world going to fall apart if they just relaxed for a bit? Is what they were saying so late on a Friday night really going to make a blind bit of difference to anyone? Surely it could wait until Monday. They can't be that important.

I believe there should be a golden rule. If a businessman has done twelve hours' work in one day he should be forced to remove his tie, switch off his computer, throw his Blackberry in a pint of beer and stop talking bollocks. Maybe they should have lorry drivers' tachometers fitted. Once they have done their allocated time or allocated amount of bullshit, they are not allowed talk anymore.

To me, it was one of those 'What the fucking hell am I doing with my life?' moments. It made me depressed. Why was I sitting in a foreign country at 9 p.m. on a Friday night, by myself?

I really hoped I wasn't like them. I hated these businessmen even though I didn't know them. They were the ones who talked loudly on their mobiles right up to the moment the plane took off. The same wankers who switched their phone back on as soon as the plane touched down. Like it was a game. Who can shoot up their phone the fastest and carry on with their boring conversation?

As I boarded the plane I made my own rule up – *Never to switch my phone on until I had cleared customs*. I knew the world wasn't going to stop or people weren't going to drop dead in the streets if no one heard my voice for another fifteen minutes. Later on I gave myself another switch-off sign: at around 7 p.m. each night, wherever I was, I put a small, black, leather bracelet on my wrist. A small thing, but in my mind it was huge. The little leather strap transported me from Anthony Griffiths, the boring consultant, to Anthony Bunko the interesting writer. It worked a treat. I simply stepped into a new and more fascinating persona. OK, it wasn't as impressive as going into a phonebox, putting my pants outside my trousers, and suddenly appearing as *Batman* or *Superman*. But it helped keep me sane, all the same. I was writer-boy!

That night I sat at the back of the plane. It was rammed full except for one seat next to me. I hoped it would be my lucky night and it would stay empty. Or, if it was going to be occupied it would be some beautiful-looking girl who insisted I took her to the toilet to join the mile high club (hopefully the girl with the Ann Summers catalogue!). But life isn't a blue movie. In my case, normally, I'd get a fat person, covered in ketchup, or some mother with a screaming baby. There is nothing worse when flying than other people's children sitting next to you, or, other people's fat people!

On one flight to Canada the guy next to me smelt of terrible body odour. He was way overweight and looked and smelled like he hadn't taken his clothes off for weeks. I didn't want to think of the state of his underpants. He smelt like a dead sheep. It got so bad I sneaked off, and, like a schoolboy, I dobbed him to the stewardess.

'Excuse me, miss... I really don't want to complain, but the man next to me is smelly.' I cringe to myself as I write what I said. But he was.

She told me to sit down and she would think of something. Minutes later she arrived with a peg for my nose. No, she didn't, but that would have been really, fucking funny. Like a true professional, she approached me and said she was sorry but there had been a mix-up, and I was in the wrong seat.

She bumped me up to business class. From BO to BC in a blink of an eye, or better still, the whiff of an armpit... what a result!

So, on that night flight home from Amsterdam I crossed my fingers that no one would sit by me. I waited with bated breath. Then I heard the shout, 'Bunko boy... how are you?'

I looked up. I couldn't believe it. There, bounding towards me like an excited puppy was a boy from my home town. Now you would have thought I would be happy to see someone I knew and at least it wasn't going to be a fat bloke, or a screaming kid. But in this case, I would have preferred the fattest man with the worst smelling armpits in the world, holding two screaming babies with the smelliest nappies ever, than to sit next to John Hope.

Now I'd known Hopey for about ten years. I'm not a close friend. He used to drink in the same pubs growing up. The thing about Hopey is, he was known for exaggerating the truth just a little, well more than a just a little if the truth be known (no pun intended). As the line in the song goes, *'if I had myself a flying giraffe... Hopey would have one in a box with a window'*.

For the entire flight he told me, and everyone else, the biggest amount of bullshit I'd ever heard in my life. And don't forget, I was a consultant. I was used to listening, and by then speaking, copious amounts of crap twenty-four hours a day.

He was on fire, even by his standards. He told me how he'd just seen the Welsh rock group, the Stereophonics, play in

Amsterdam to ten thousand fans. Halfway through their set, he said Kelly Jones (the singer) stopped the concert and shouted out, 'Hey, Hopey boy, how's it going?'

Now that was the type of shit he was feeding me.

He also told me he met Rick Wakeman, who, also, somehow fucking knew him, and had invited him to a party.

By then I lost the will to live.

'Did you know I have been picked to captain the Dutch national rugby side?' How he kept a straight fucking face was beyond me.

I could see people slyly glancing at us. I wanted to stand up and shout, 'I don't know him... honest.'

As we were heading towards Cardiff airport, our plane hit some turbulence. Lightning hit the plane. The plane bounced about and then sharply dropped. I screamed. Hopey didn't stop for breath. He carried on lying.

'God,' I said a silent prayer, 'what did I do so badly in my life to have deserved my last hour to have been sat next to this twat?'

We finally landed. 'Thank you, God,' I muttered.

All the businessmen switched their phones on to tell someone they had just landed. Hopey asked me if I would give him a lift home from the airport. I looked up. 'God, you twat.'

13

The Country that Always Eats

AFTER SPENDING MOST of my time in the coldest parts of Europe, catching scabies while staying in some of the foulest hotels known to man, I'd had enough. So when I was asked if I fancied spending a few months working in the States, my suitcase was almost packed before putting the phone down.

'Only in America', Bono, singer, and part-time choirboy, of supergroup U2, once said on picking up a hideous pair of crocodile boots in a TV documentary I watched ages ago. I didn't know exactly what he meant back then, but that all changed after spending time in the country that always eats.

I flew business class for the first time. Smirking at all the peasants in cattle-class, I strolled past them waving my golden ticket. While they ate from pig troughs, I sat watching my very own TV, nibbling on strange prawn things and drinking copious amounts of good quality wine. It was like a dream come true, for a while.

On landing in New York I had a tight connection time to get my next flight to Cleveland. Two hours in fact, in which twenty precious minutes had already been lost while waiting for a 'large' American gentleman in a cowboy hat – who looked as if he had two midgets fighting to the death in his sweat pants – to get forklifted out of his seat.

When I eventually got off the plane, I walked past a line of wheelchairs. There must have been about fifteen of them. I wasn't sure what they were for. Maybe the entire Paralympic team were on board and I hadn't seen them? Or, perhaps, a shed load of handicapped kids were on their way to Disneyland in Florida.

Not even close. The wheelchairs were used to transport
the disabled, aka fat, people with enormous butts around the
terminal. An army of airport staff waited to move these so-
called handicapped humans from A to B. They all sat there like
whales on a beach.

I wanted to yell out, 'Let them walk, the exercise will do
them good.'

Little did I know there was method in their laziness. I shook
my head and carried on walking.

'Welcome to America', the sign in Newark airport
announced. What was missing underneath were the words:
*'Now you must queue up in the biggest line in the world with
the rest of the illegal immigrants.'*

I couldn't believe the queue of people lined up in front of
me. At first I thought something had gone wrong up ahead.
Maybe someone had collapsed, or Midget-Fighting-Arse Sweat
Pants Man had got lodged in a doorway, and they were trying
to bulldoze him out.

'What's wrong?' I asked a lady.

'Nothing... this is the queue to get through passport
control.'

I thought it was a joke. I'd sat for eight hours on a plane
and now I had to wait in this. I'm not exaggerating when I
say the line was longer than the one in Disneyland to get on
Terror Towers. At least at Disney there's a monitor, or a Disney
character, to entertain the crowds. Here there was only a trigger-
happy police officer, who wouldn't have smiled if he had won
the lottery, and his albino sniffer dog. White from head to toe,
even the creature's eyeballs were white, or maybe he had just
found a bag of coke. The beast sniffed me vigorously for a full
five minutes before moving off.

I got more pissed off when I saw the wheelchairs' brigade
waltzing past me and straight to the front of the queue. What
made it worse was the fat 'disabled' people had hundreds of
family members prancing behind them like freeloaders getting
into a nightclub with a superstar. Without being funny, I was

sure one of the ladies in a wheelchair was actually dead. I could see one of her family members walking behind her, moving her arms and mouth with pieces of string, like a puppet.

And what's more, I counted thirty empty passport booths which could have been manned that morning. How many were actually manned? Six! And the guy in one of them worked so slowly he should have had a snail-shell on his back.

I stood there tamping. Time quickly ticking away. I had about forty-five minutes, and I still had to get my luggage and get to terminal C, wherever the fuck that was. And knowing my luck, I would get stopped and searched. I know I look like an extra off *Crimewatch*, because it had got to the point where I got stopped at least once in every trip. Always the same routine, stopped, searched, knock my computer on. Take my shoes off. Jump on one leg and put my left hand in, and left hand out. It was ridiculous.

Whatever happened, the deadpan airport security guards and their weird-looking sniffer dogs always made a beeline for me. I'm positive if I had a shade darker skin, security guards would have blown me up while I sat in the terminal eating some sushi, waiting for my gate to open.

I imagined them whispering, while hiding behind a fake bush.

'He's got a bomb?'

'No, Boss, it looks like a salmon roll.'

'Never mind what it is... never trust a terrorist who eats fish... blow the fucker up.'

BOOOOOMMMM!

In Newark, I hurriedly shuffled forward and smiled nervously at the large guy sitting behind the glass counter. He didn't smile back, just scanned my passport. I'm not sure why they treat everyone as if we are a cross between Bin Laden, Hitler and Keith Richards. Why is it, when someone gets a job doing security at an airport they suddenly turn into anti-social beings?

I felt as if I was a convict getting interviewed for a murder.

'Why have you been to Turkey?' he looked at the stamp on the pages.

'Holidays,' I smiled.

He glared at me, and ticked some form.

'And why have you been to Greece, Spain, France... Egypt?'

I wanted to say, 'Because unlike you lot, in Europe we like to travel around to other countries, enjoy their cultures, and, by the way, that doesn't mean bombing the fuck out of them.' Instead, I again said, 'Holidays.'

'Are you a no-good, slimy Arab terrorist?' he yelled at me. OK, he didn't, but that's what he was thinking. 'Have a nice day,' he actually grunted through clenched teeth and handed my stuff back.

The best story I've ever heard was when Joe went to the States to run a workshop a few years later. At Newark airport he showed his passport, and suddenly got surrounded by armed police. They carted him off to a cell. He didn't know what the hell was going on. Several police officers interviewed him for well over two hours. When they let him go they apologised but explained to him he had the same name, and the same birthday, as another Joe Williams who was on America's most wanted list for murder and other crimes.

Joe realised their concern and fully understood the action they took. Well, that was until he searched his most infamous namesake on Google when he got back. He found out Joe Williams the murderer was about seventeen stone (Joe the consultant was twelve, soaking wet), the murderer had an afro (Joe had straight fair hair) and best of all, and still unbelievably, the criminal was black. And not just a bit black, very, very black. Joe the consultant was a very, very white, forty-year-old who probably hadn't had any contact with a black person until around 1994.

When he told me, I pictured the conversation between the security guards looking through the two-way mirror at a very scared, confused and white Joe.

'Are you sure it's our man?'

'Must be... he's got the same name and same date of birth.'

'Isn't he a bit white to be the man we are looking for?'

'Disguise... haven't you seen Eddie Murphy in *Coming to America*? He plays those three white barber guys... and you would swear he was white if he didn't look so black.'

Unbelievable! I know! But that's Americans for you!

Rushing through Newark airport, I only just made the connecting flight. On the much smaller plane I sat next to the wing, looking out at the gang of baggage handlers throwing suitcases onto the conveyor. Initially, I couldn't see my suitcase. 'Fuck here we go. Canada all over again,' I thought, in reference to the occasion my case got lost while travelling through Schiphol airport to Toronto a year before. I had been there for five days and didn't get my luggage until the last day. And then, they lost it on the return journey.

At least I didn't have that problem on my US trip. I spied my well-worn blue suitcase slowly snaking its way up the moving conveyor. At last I could relax. I kicked off my Converse trainers and sat back.

Then, two army trucks pulled up. 'Strange,' I thought. Several soldiers hopped out, dressed in full uniform. Some of them stood to attention by the conveyor. The others opened the back of the other truck and slid out a coffin, draped in the Stars and Stripes flag. The body of a dead soldier who, I assumed, had been killed in action. I sat stunned. They proceeded to put it on the conveyor. I watched it move slowly up the ramp while they stood to attention. Out of respect I made the sign of the cross, but then slyly snapped a photo of it on my phone to show my mates when I got back home.

My thoughts drifted back to the poor soldier and I began to wonder how he had died. Sniper fire? Landmine made from coke cans? Dynamite strapped to a stray goat? There were so many ingenious ways terrorists got their man nowadays. Yet, however it happened it was a bad show, that poor soldier, who had lost his life fighting for some lost cause, was getting transported back to his family in the undercarriage of a plane among all the suitcases, stuffed animals and other paraphernalia.

After another wine or two my imagination transported me to the possible scene when we arrived at the other end.

I'm waiting for my luggage to appear on the carousel. The odd suitcase rolls in through the opening and then out pops the coffin of the dead soldier. In my mind's eye I watch his father and younger brother clambering over people struggling to get it off the moving conveyor. As they start carrying it away, the mother looks at the tag on it. 'Oh hang on... this isn't our Chuck, this is some other Chuck... put it back you idiots,' she barks at the father. The men struggle to put it back on, while another grieving family wait around the bend of the conveyor belt.

Of course, I never saw the coffin when we landed. Whisked off, like a stone-dead rock star in its own ice-cold limo. What I did see though was some weird-looking bloke holding up a card with my name on it. Al Jones was that bloke.

Mad Al, as I instantly labelled him, was my designated driver for the week and was also on the course I was running at the steel mill. A very peculiar-looking herb, and that's coming from a person who grew up in a town with its fair share of weird-looking herbs. If, for some bizarre reason, I had been asked to describe Mad Al to the police investigating a series of murders or maybe I was writing a character for a book about Hobbits and other creatures, this is how I would have portrayed him. If the mental family from the film *Texas Chain Saw Massacre* had a weird in-bred brother they were a bit ashamed of and hid in the attic because he kept frightening Leatherface, Mad Al would have been him.

On my life, I'm sure he was bald but had sewn real hair into the edges of his baseball cap, which he never took off. I wondered whose hair it was. I hoped it wasn't another Lean consultant he'd fallen in love with and still had parts of him tied up to a bedpost in his basement, right opposite his dead mother and the scalped heads of other victims.

Even our small talk on the hour-long drive from the airport proved weird. He kept insisting his distant relatives were from 'Whales'... which he assured me was just off the coast of Iceland, or somewhere over that way. I didn't want to argue.

To give me time to unwind, and acclimatise to my new surroundings, I'd travelled out on the Saturday. We rolled into town around 6 p.m. I politely refused a drink with Mad Al in his local called the Wagon Wheel. He smiled as he told me with pride that tonight was singles' night and the bar was famous not only for its spicy chicken wings, but also for its barmaid with no teeth giving out blow-jobs in the car park after ten (or it could have been to ten customers, I didn't want to ask). To be honest after all the stress of flying, queuing up in endless lines, getting questioned, rushing for my connecting planes, and the episode with the dead soldier, I could have done with a relaxing gobble. But there was no way in a million years I was going to put my dick in some woman's mouth (teeth or no teeth), who may have once had her laughing gear anywhere near Mad Al's small, hairy (or probably bald with fake hair around the edges) todger.

Instead I checked in to my Holiday Inn hotel. I put my feet up, and decided to sample some American TV. Another of my 'only in America' moments. In Britain, adverts are slotted in between TV programmes. In America, sadly, TV programmes are briefly slotted in between adverts. I settled down to watch *Scarface*. Four hours later, and Al Pacino still hadn't introduced the drug gangs to his little friend! But I had, however, been brainwashed into thinking I needed Viagra to boost my love life. Mama's famous pizzas were really the best pizzas in town. And, apparently, I hadn't lived because I hadn't eaten an entire bucket-load of greasy, chicken wings from Smokey's Bar and Grill for two dollars forty cents.

A constant bombardment of selling and fast food. But that was nothing compared to when I tuned in on the Sunday morning. I sat in bed staring, open-mouthed, at the religious channels. The most unreal and surreal thing I'd ever seen in my life. One religious demi-god must have been about 165 years old if a day. His wig kept falling down his face as he told me and the other stupid idiots watching that *we were all doooooomed*. Someone must have been employed to push his wig back in place during the commercial breaks. I lay there speechless, flicking from nutcase channel to nutcase channel. One good-looking guy preached in a football stadium. Seventy thousand religious fanatics hollered at his every word. He raced across the glittering altar like Mick Jagger at Wembley. I just couldn't imagine my old priest, Father Clancy, doing that. His hands shook giving out the communion, never mind an encore of the Lord's Prayer while juggling the lit candles.

After swearing on the Bible I found in the drawer that I would never go to church ever again, I needed sustenance. Downstairs I asked at reception where the nearest restaurant was.

'About half a mile sir,' she drawled. 'Have you got a car, or do you want me to organise the courtesy bus... it will take about fifteen minutes.'

'No it's OK... I'll walk.'

My reply was met with a stunned silence. People behind me nudged and whispered to one another. 'He's going to walk.' The woman's eyebrows raised up in terror.

I strolled out, whistling to myself. People in their cars actually slowed down to stare at me. Imagine the conversation when they got home.

Darling, you won't believe what I saw today... a man walking.

By himself... using his legs?

Yeah... honest... just strolling across the road, down to the shops... he didn't stop for fast food, or oxygen... or Viagra!

You better phone the sheriff... there's a nutcase on the loose.

With my morning exercise out of the way, I ended up in

a place called Daman's. A typical American bar, with more TVs on the wall than in the entire warehouse of Radio Rentals. All the TVs showed the kind of sport which I, and most other people in the world, have no interest in at all. It was distracting, but the food was great, very unhealthy, and way too much. But hey, sometimes when in Rome, eat like an overweight American. Ever since that first meal, I developed a bit of a Pavlov's dog thing whenever I landed in the States. Even today, if I go to America (or even walk passed TGI Fridays), my mouth instantly salivates for chicken tenders, loaded potato skins, a river of ranch dressing and a pint of ice cold lager served in a frosted glass. Nothing else will do.

The restaurant was full to the point of bursting. I know everyone says all Americans are fat, in a generalised kind of way, but most of them bloody well are, and no wonder. Wedged in the table next to me, sat the fattest person I had ever seen. She must have been about forty-five stone. My kid's life, her head was the same size and shape as a beanbag from Argos. She had rolls of fat on her chin bigger than my thighs.

In front of her, plates and plates of food waited to be eaten. Waitresses, like excited Dalmatian pups, returned to her table every two seconds with more. It was sadder than the sight of the dead soldier at the airport. I wanted to jump up and fire a gun in the air, my bullets splatting into the ceiling tiles. But I didn't have a gun, and I thought throwing a bread roll wouldn't have the same impact. I just wanted to yell out. 'For fuck's sake, can't you see you're killing this poor beast? Stop giving her food. If she was a heroin addict you wouldn't give her a pack of brown smack and a small spoon.'

Bizarrely, a month later I went back to the same place, and the same woman sat at the same table, in the same clothes. Only difference was her face had got fatter, or her eyes had shrunk. I assumed she was now just too heavy to leave. Maybe she had come in there months before when she was only a mere pup at thirty-odd stones, and ate and ate, and now she couldn't get out. I imagined the waitresses placing a blanket over her head as they locked up and knocked the lights off at the end of their shift.

'Bye, Doris, see you in the morning.'

The more I ventured to the States, the more I'm now convinced that the way Bin Laden would have brought down American society was just to hide out in a cave for another ten years until everyone in America was too fat and too lazy to fight. In fact, the head of Al Qaeda shouldn't have directed the planes into the Twin Towers. No way – he should have had them fly into all the fast-food places in the States. That would have caused more panic on the streets of New York. The place would have come to a complete standstill.

Anyway, nice and relaxed after my Sunday, Mad Al turned up for me at 5.30 on Monday morning. Driving to the factory, I felt a little nervous. It was like playing the first game of rugby of the season. Butterflies flapped about in my stomach and adrenaline rushed through my veins.

During our journey to the plant he pulled over into a Dunkin' Donut roadside shop. Not only was there a queue of cars waiting at the drive-through, but the car park was also full. Mad Al got out and disappeared into the shop. I presumed he stopped to get us some coffee. He did appear with two cups of coffee and carried two massive boxes. He put them in the boot (or since we were in America, the trunk).

At the factory, I set up my stuff, had a quick toilet break, and waited for my prey, sorry guests, to arrive. At 6 a.m. sharp, they piled in. Mad Al brought in the two boxes. They were crammed with donuts.

I have never seen donuts like them. Massive, genetically engineered donuts... Jurassic Park of the donut world. If one had rolled off the table, it would have flattened the gatehouse and everything in its path. Packed full of calories, with enough jam and icing sugar to cover a small elephant. I'm sure Elvis Presley at the height of his 'twenty-thousand calorie sandwich a day' addiction would have struggled to eat half of one.

It didn't stop the employees. They munched away like a man

about to be sent to the electric chair. I waited and waited for them to finish. How the hell was I going to get them motivated enough to go and clean a rolling steel mill? All I would want to do after eating one of those would be to curl up by the fire, put the TV on, and watch some adverts. Furthermore, they had donuts every morning that week, except for Thursday when it was breakfast pizza morning. I won't ever take you there.

Nevertheless, finally we started, but only after another coffee refill and then they decided on what they wanted for lunch. There was a show of hands to decide if it should be philly steaks or pizza. In the end they agreed on both, with bags of French fries, and the token green salad to make them feel good.

The aim for the workshop was to try and improve the performance of one of their rolling mills, which is a big machine which rolled steel. (That's enough of the technical stuff. Told you I wasn't suited to this.)

One guy disappeared to the toilet, so I said to the group. 'OK, everyone… we'll start when the coloured guy comes back.'

Fuckin' hell, if I had. I wasn't trying to be disrespectful – the opposite actually. Where I came from, in my little Welsh village, I honestly thought calling someone black would be more offensive. I was so, so wrong. It was like that famous scene from *American Werewolf in London*, but renamed, the 'Stupid Welsh Twat in Ohio'. One guy drinking hot coffee missed his mouth, dribbling liquid down the front of his shirt. 'I've been drinking coffee for forty-five years and I've never missed my mouth before,' he stated.

They all stared at me. I honestly thought they were going to beat me up, or eat me.

I apologised for my ignorance. They grunted. I quickly changed the subject by explaining what we were going to do that week. After a short while they started to come around. They asked many questions and came up with lots of suggestions and improvement ideas.

'This is going to be a walk in the park,' I thought. But life isn't as easy as that. There is always a big, steaming pile of dog shit to step in along the way.

Everything was about to change dramatically.

About an hour into the training, the door burst open. In walked Ray. Mad Al had warned me about Insane Ray. With all these characters it was beginning to sound like a typical Monday afternoon at Wetherspoon's. All they needed was Malcolm Knuckles, Ronny Mouthorgan and Alan the Midget and the gang would have been complete.

Insane Ray, with one leg shorter than the other, was the only black chargehand at the mill. Word on the grapevine was he possessed two massive chips on each shoulder and a head full of hatred. A troublemaker prone to pulling out the racial card if things didn't go his way.

I could sense everyone's mood changing as soon as he hobbled in.

I strolled over. 'Hello, Ray.' I held my hand out. 'I'm Anthony... Thanks for coming.'

He looked at me as though I was a piece of shit on his shoe. He brushed past and slumped down in the seat. I kept my cool. I focused on keeping the group on track. Before lunch we went out and looked at the machine. When we came back, I used an old consultant trick and split them into pairs to do some work. 'Divide and conquer,' The Master often drummed into me.

I got some of the team members to clean out the mill. Others I got to fix any broken items on the machines. While a few collected data on things like breakdowns, speeds and major quality issues.

By the afternoon, even Insane Ray came around, a little. He even spoke to me.

'I got you, you bastard,' I thought, smirking to myself. I poured him a mug of coffee.

I started believing I was a good consultant after all. 'Ray, what do you think of this?' I showed him some of the data we had found on why they were having such poor quality on the mill.

On his mill!

Big, big mistake. He took it all very personally. A slur on his leadership. All my good work and I was back to square one. Ray switched off and stopped getting involved in anything at all. He sat on his chair, face like thunder.

It suddenly became a long, long afternoon. By the end of the day I needed a drink. Mad Al had arranged a few beers for all the team later in the Wagon Wheel. Luckily, the waitress with no teeth had the night off. Looking after her twelve kids in a trailer, I assumed.

When I turned up at the pub I could feel tension in the air. Insane Ray sat by the bar, obviously a little worse for wear. 'Work is work, play is play,' is my motto. I went over to shake his hand. He pushed my hand away and ignored me. Two French-Canadian guys who had come down especially to be part of the week's event from a sister company saw what was going on and called me over. A few drinks later we retired into another room for a bite to eat. Insane Ray didn't join us. He stayed at the bar, drinking.

It was a typical spit and sawdust, chicken and rib place. The team let their hair down and we were having a good laugh. All of a sudden, halfway through our main meal, I felt someone looming over me.

'You are a racist!' Insane Ray drunkenly grunted in my direction.

'What?'

'You... you're a fuckin' racist!'

That was it, my blood reached boiling point. 'Hang on now, Ray... I'm not a racist.' I eyeballed him back. To be honest, he was a hard-looking bastard, packed full of muscle, with a three-inch scar running down from his eye to his cheek. All I had was an appendix scar, and an odd-looking thumb from an old rugby injury.

'Prove it,' he yelled.

Everything in the place stopped. I'm sure even the cooks stuck their head out of the kitchen.

What the hell was he talking about? What did he expect me to do? Pull out a card which said, 'Anthony is not a racist', or produce a letter off one of my black friends back home. 'Look, Ray, I'm not... I don't know what the hell you're talking about,' I added.

'Come with me then Mister Big-shot, and prove it. I want you to fuck a big, black woman... come on, you racist.'

Part of me was already picturing me on an old rickety bed back-scuttling some black mama with titties the size of over-ripe melons. I quickly shook it out of my brain. 'Don't be so stupid,' I replied.

One of his work colleagues tried to pull him away. Insane Ray kept staring at me. Then the twat spat in my food. A big fuck-off greenie with extra bits in it... bits of carrot... and other unmentionable substances.

That was it. It was war. Luckily my two Canadian friends dragged me away and we left.

Next morning, a Mexican stand-off took place: Ray out on the machine by himself, and me and the others in the office. In the end, I called the event off when the management team decided that the best thing was to leave Ray alone in case he put in a grievance.

'Grievance,' I slammed the table, 'he spat a greenie in my food.'

'We don't want to provoke him. He's retiring in two years.'

I shook my head in amazement. The Canadian guys had heard enough. They flew home that day. We carried on working for the week but on another machine as far away as we could from Insane fuckin' Ray and his rolling mill.

For me it was the worst experience I'd had so far in my consultant life. I couldn't wait to get home. I'd had enough of all their hassle, their crappy TV, and insane chargehands spitting in my food.

However, surely, I thought if I travelled to the States a million more times nothing could ever go as badly as that again. How wrong could I be?

15

Murder in New York

ONE OF THE most frustrating things about most Americans is their complete ignorance about the rest of the world. When they asked me where I was from, I may as well have said 'Mars', because ninety-nine point nine per cent of them didn't have a clue what I was talking about when I said 'Wales'.

'Wales.' I tried to explain. 'It's in the UK.' Blank looks came back at me every time. 'Have you heard of Tom Jones?' I would add.

'Ohhhh, we love Tom Jones,' they would reply, 'and Benny Hill.'

'OK... so Tom Jones is from Wales. I haven't got a bloody clue where Benny Hill is from... probably Kansas.'

Lots of the Americans thought my accent was Australian. One girl in a bar came up with the best one yet.

'Are you from Greenland?' she blurted out.

Everyone in the bar stared at me as if I was a circus freak.

'That bloke is from Greenland,' I heard someone else whisper.

Why the hell did she think I was from Greenland? Did she know anyone from Greenland? Had she seen anyone from Greenland? Has anyone ever seen anyone from fucking Greenland? Do people actually live in fucking Greenland? Does it exist? Is it bloody green?

During one trip I decided to test their lack of knowledge. During a session with a group of middle managers I gave them a geography lesson. On a flip chart I drew the British Isles and split it into the four countries. I didn't want to confuse them even more by splitting Ireland in two. I asked them to name the four countries that made up the UK.

They all knew Scotland. I think it was because of Mel Gibson's film *Braveheart*, and the golf. Ireland came out next. They weren't sure which part of the map it was, but they had all downed a pint of green lager (which they dyed especially) on Saint Paddy's day. For some reason a bigger event in America than in Ireland.

'OK... the last two,' I asked.

Now they struggled. They looked at each other.

Looking back now it would have been funny if someone had said 'Greenland'. I probably would have said, 'Yes, it is Greenland and the last one is Mongo McBongo.'

'London,' someone muttered. The rest nodded in agreement.

Incredibly, they thought London was a country. And these were not low-level employees making battery parts on presses on the shop floor. They were high-flying managers in well-paid, respected jobs.

One guy in the sales office actually came from Wales. He had been living there for a year or so. He told me a story about when he and his family went out to a restaurant in their small town. The waitress serving them was really friendly. She asked the children their names and all the other kind of stuff they do when looking for a good tip.

She brought more coffee and said, 'I love your accent; where are you guys from?'

'Great Britain,' the sales guy replied.

'Wow, that's amazing,' she added, 'how long have you been over here?'

'Nearly three months.'

Without blinking an eyelash, she added, 'Gosh... and you have all picked up the language in such a short time... that's awesome!'

I rest my case. Only in America!

Nevertheless I did do some really cool stuff, as well, on the trip. I went to a shooting gallery one night after work. Bloody hell, it was loud, but I must admit, good fun. However, I'm really glad there are gun laws in the UK. If there hadn't been, I imagine most of my mates, including me, would probably be dead by now. And that's not exaggerating. A Friday night in the Brandy Bridge nightclub in Merthyr, with people tanked up on Special Brew, would have ended up like *High Noon* meets *Scarface* with gunshots ricocheting off the walls.

On one of my last occasions in the States, I was in the middle of writing a spoof TV cartoon pilot about life on a mental housing estate. I told someone about it in the steel mill. Their uncle happened to be a policeman and he asked if I fancied going out with him one night on patrol. One of the areas he covered was 'The Projects', the name given to the American version of our rough council housing estates.

It sounded a million times more exciting than cleaning a big steel mill machine from six in the morning until six at night.

I couldn't wait to go. Although, I didn't tell any of my family, or work colleagues back home what I was doing. Knowing my mother, she would have been over on the next plane to stop me.

So, late one Wednesday night, Todd, the cop, arrived at my hotel in his patrol car at around 10.30. A full-on, Yank-style TV copper with muscles bugling everywhere but also a bit of a donut-belly protruding out of his shirt.

We cruised around for about five minutes. It felt like real *Starsky and Hutch* stuff. I thought back to the Starsky jumper my mother knitted me when I was young. I begged her for it, but, in the end, I never wore it. It looked good on Paul Michael Glaser as he fought crime on the streets of California. It didn't have the same effect for an eleven-year-old boy running around Dowlais Flats in the rain.

I might have guessed our first stop of the night would be at a coffee shop. Todd grabbed us a couple of large coffees and a few donuts. Three cops were already sat at the table when we arrived. They stared at me as I introduced myself in my torn jeans, Converse boots and army jacket.

I didn't dare tell them that I was writing a spoof cartoon show about a mental housing estate with corrupt, donut-bellied cops. Instead, I lied. 'I'm writing a short story about the dangers the police face on a daily basis.'

I hoped my contact hadn't told them the truth.

After another drink, we headed off. I felt excited, but a little nervous. I had never been that close to someone carrying a gun (or guns) before. The cop had one in his belt and a big fuck-off Gatling gun contraption strapped to his car. I sat in the passenger seat, with my notepad on my lap, trying to look like a real writer.

We drove slowly around The Projects. It looked a mean, eerily unforgiving place. A place, I imagined, that housed the lost souls of life.

We turned a corner into a long, dark street. Three guys stood in the middle of the road acting suspiciously. Todd switched on the flashing lights. I took a deep breath. This was the real deal. With their heads down, two of the guys dashed off down an alleyway. The other guy stood there staring directly back at the car.

We pulled up alongside him. Todd wound the window down. My heart beat wildly in my chest.

'What you doing?' he said to the man. It sounded like he knew him.

The man, face full of stubble, staggered up to the window. He wore a long, dirty raincoat.

'Put your hands where I can see them,' Todd barked.

The man leaned in. He glared at me with dark piercing eyes. 'Who's he?' he asked the policeman. I could smell the alcohol on his breath from where I was.

'CIA,' the cop replied.

I stared at the man, giving him my best 'hard' stare. Then I thought, 'Fuck what if he's got a massive gun under that coat? What if he's high on crack? What if he hates CIA men because they killed his old man, or his best friend, or his dog? Worse still, what if he recognises me from some crap consultant workshop I'd run in a previous life?' Perhaps I had given his company some advice and they had gone bust, and that's why he was living on the street, and selling wraps of crack.

I wish I hadn't come.

After a few questions, Todd told him to get home, or he would run him in. The man gave me an even harder stare, and then disappeared. I finally breathed out. My hands shook too much to write anything down.

A while later a call came through about a disturbance in another part of The Projects. Todd sped through the side streets, his lights again flashing. Within minutes, we arrived at the scene. Another cop car was already parked up. Two guys stood toe-to-toe in the middle of the street fighting. A gang of people hung about watching.

'Out,' Todd said to me.

'What?'

'Out... stand over there.' He pointed to a row of houses, 'Just stay by the lamp post and don't talk to anyone.'

'What?'

'Over there,' he pointed.

I honestly didn't want to get out of the safety of the car. This was now too real for me. Fuck the spoof thing. I'd had enough. I wanted to go back to my hotel. Or at least stay in the car and not talk to anyone. But I did what I was told.

Todd and the other cop got among the crowd trying to cool the situation down.

I suddenly felt very, very alone. Black faces surrounded me. The guy in the dirty raincoat we had stopped earlier, stood among them. He glared at me, a smirk on his face.

'Fucking hell,' I thought, 'all I need is for Insane Ray to pop up with that big, black woman he wanted me to hump and I would be truly fucked.'

A little part of me thought maybe the cops had set it all up. Maybe they were going to drive off and leave me there. A cop's prank! A way of showing the cocky writer boy from Greenland, or wherever I was from, that they were the boss. Perhaps they were secretly taping it. I would be on the cop version of *Punk'd*. (*Cop'd*.)

But the way one of the coppers smashed one of the fighters into the bonnet of a car, I knew it wasn't a set-up. It was a true life-or-death situation. I thought about legging it. But I couldn't move. My legs hardly held my own weight. I backed slowly towards the car.

The man in the dirty overcoat stepped towards me. I tried not to look scared although I was petrified. Luckily, Todd sorted the disturbance out and came to my rescue. Everyone in the street sloped off back into their houses, or crack dens, or cardboard boxes. I didn't care as long as they weren't around me.

'Let's go for a snack,' Todd said.

I have never been so happy to sit in a coffee bar eating a donut in my entire life.

*

However, it was while travelling home from that same trip to America that I had my worst experience ever. It started the night before I flew. It snowed heavily in the Cleveland area, and I just about managed to get to my hotel.

The snow came down for hours. Nothing moved in the city at all. No cars, trains or planes. There was absolute mayhem in my hotel. The reception area was rammed full of young kids and soccer parents. (The most annoying kind of Americans, bar none. Loud, badly dressed, large hair and smiley teeth like Champion, the Wonder Horse.) To make matters worse, all the delis in the area had closed. The hotel didn't have a kitchen. I sat there watching twenty-stone people racing, well not racing, waddling as fast as they could around, panicking because they couldn't get anything to eat. The fattest kids I had ever seen lay on the floor, screaming and clutching their stomachs. On my life, with the amount of blubber they were carrying they could have lasted without food for about six months. A fucking camel would have died before most of them.

I sat by the fire, writing, and eating a packet of Quavers I'd found in my bag. Everything went quiet. I turned around. All eyes stared at me. One mother I'm sure had been sneaking up on me to try to snatch them. I was surrounded by a big gang of Quaver-hungry zombies. I teased them with every bite, until the point I thought they were going to rip the bag out of my hands, eat them, and probably eat me, straight after.

I quickly went to bed to watch some adverts (all containing food and Viagra!).

Unbelievably, the morning after, the snow almost disappeared. I got to the airport and boarded the plane. All systems ready to go to get back home to God's country, via New York. Then I heard the following announcement.

'Sorry, there's been a further delay,' the captain of the plane in Cleveland informed us. 'Trouble in Newark.'

'Oh, fuck it,' I muttered.

'Sorry, folks, we are doing our best,' the captain said. It was followed by him giving the stewardess instructions, after he thought he had turned the intercom off. 'Hey, Doris, you better push out the boat and give them two packs of pretzels, looks like we are here for a while.'

'Great,' I thought. 'Another four hours of my life wasted.'

If I didn't feel like slitting my wrists at that moment, I definitely did a few minutes later. I reached into my bag for my iPod to lock the world out. As I mentioned, I'm not the best conversationalist in the world, even with people I know and like. So why individuals think it necessary to disclose their life story to a complete stranger on a plane is beyond me.

I dropped the earplugs on the floor. I hoped no one noticed but, too late, I got spotted. Next to me, a rather tanned man sat in shorts. Yes, shorts! It was fucking freezing outside and this guy wore khaki cream shorts and Indian beads around his neck. He zoomed in on me.

'It can't be helped.' He smiled at me through a set of teeth normally connected to the jaws of a lion.

I knew straight away I was in trouble. He clutched a well-worn Bible in his hands. Why did I always attract weirdos like this? I must be like a man-sized neon light attracting every psychopathic moth in the street.

I tried to look occupied by staring out of the window. I prayed he would go away. But hell no! His religious hooks tore deep into my flesh, and he wasn't letting me go. He tapped my shoulder, 'Do you travel often?'

I wished they hadn't confiscated my trusty old lump hammer at customs.

Through clenched teeth I entered into some small talk. He turned out to be so religious he should have had a fucking halo dangling over his curly hair. He'd just come back from doing missionary work in Africa for the last few years. By the way, how do people get away with becoming missionaries in the first place? Do they study it in school? Do they go to some foreign, poor country on a cheap holiday, and like it so much that they stay there? Or are they born to do it? I pictured myself going to tell my father I was leaving school, and going to spread the word of God, and become a missionary.

'Yeah, right,' I could just hear my father's sarcastic reply. 'And I'm going to give up my job and play for Manchester United. Now get up those stairs and tidy your room. Missionary? I blame your mother's side of the family. They were all mental.'

But I was trapped like a sardine in a can. The nutcase happily told me all about making mud huts, and digging drainage holes with his bare hands, and whatever else missionaries do. He brought out photos, and even sung me the village song, which they only sang if they caught a wild boar or a rare bat or a dinosaur. Even though we hadn't moved an inch in two hours, I wondered if I could fake travel sickness. In fact, I did really want to spew into the bag.

He talked, and talked, and talked.

I am not violent, but I felt like jabbing a pretzel in his eye. I would have, if I hadn't eaten them because I was starving. After four and a half hours of listening to Holy Moses, the plane finally took off. As soon as we were in the air I plugged my in-house entertainment system in, and settled down to have some quality time for myself. Thirty minutes into the flight we hit the worst turbulence I have ever known. The stewardesses whooshed around like rag dolls.

'I'm going to die,' I thought, 'Thank you, God. Last time this happened, I spent my time listening to Hopey from Merthyr, and now I've just spent my last four hours listening to some religious maniac telling me more unwanted stories.' Then it hit me, 'Hang on, if he is really that close to God, maybe if we do crash, he will survive.' I edged in a little closer to him. He took my hand, honest to God, and said, 'Don't worry... this is nothing. When I was in Africa, I was chased by an elephant... and...'

'Stewardess,' I cried out, 'bring me a fucking gun or a fresh bag of fucking pretzels.'

After the delay in Cleveland, naturally, on arriving at Newark, not only had my plane fucked off, but every single member of BA staff had fucked off for the night as well. They had simply closed up shop as though it was a bank holiday. All that was missing, as I stood shaking, looking at the spot where the booking clerk should have been sitting, was a sign saying: *Gone home, back in morning, if you need us, sorry, you are screwed... ha ha... Have a nice day!*'

I actually screamed out loud in the empty departure hall. Screamed at the top of my lungs. The last few stragglers carrying suitcases stopped for a few seconds to stare at the mad Welshman bawling at the top of his voice.

'Flights must be cancelled to Greenland,' I'm sure one of them muttered.

They looked pitifully at me before carrying on. I'm not too ashamed to admit, I cried. Tears rolled down my face. It was 11.30 p.m. in Newark airport, I'd missed my flight, I had earache, nowhere to stay, I couldn't find my luggage, and I was all alone. The only thing I had on my person was my computer bag draped over my shoulder.

Luckily, a woman working on the Continental airlines desk took pity on me. She went out of her way to sort out a return flight for the next morning. She also booked me a motel, about two miles away. She didn't need to do it, but she did. She was my knight in blue and yellow uniform.

Thinking my nightmare had finished, I headed outside. Alas, it had only just begun.

I had a feeling straightaway, as I waited in the taxi line, that the driver who was lined up to take me was a little odd. He just looked really peculiar. His eyes were way too close together, narrow pointy features that belonged on the face of a hitman. As I got nearer the front, he started waving at me. I ignored him.

'Where you going?' the attendant at the head of the line taking names asked me.

I told him the motel. 'That will be twenty bucks,' he said and wrote down the cab's number onto his pad. He told the taxi driver my destination and the price.

I could see by the driver's face he wasn't happy. We'd only just pulled out of the airport when he turned around to face me. 'That will be fifty dollars,' he spat his words out in a harsh-sounding, pigeon English.

'What?'

'Fifty dollars.'

He stared at me through the rear-view mirror, his face screwed up and his eyes full of hate. I tried to explain politely that I was positive the guy at the taxi rank, who I now assumed was employed to make sure innocent tourists didn't get ripped off by insane-looking taxi drivers, told us both it would be twenty dollars to take me from the airport terminal to the motel. But the Eastern European-looking driver wasn't listening to a word I said. Instead, he slammed the brakes on. The cab came to a sudden stop on the dark slip-road leading out of Newark airport. Off in the distance the lights of New York City sparkled.

'Fifty, or you get out here,' a hint of desperation in his voice but, sadly for me, he held all the aces. I held fuck-all, except my passport and a packet of extra strong mints.

I knew I was being taken for a ride, not just in a physical sense, but, to be truthful, why should I care what he charged? My business would foot the bill anyway. I just needed somewhere to crash for a few hours.

So I sat in the back of the taxi with the mad guy with evil eyes, the cab still motionless, the engine purring away.

'OK... OK... fifty bucks,' I replied.

Eventually, we continued on our journey. I stared out of the window as we drove. How rough the streets appeared surprised me. Tramps and prostitutes everywhere I looked. A police car shot past going in the opposite direction. I checked the time. We had been driving for a good ten minutes. I was confused. The woman in the terminal definitely said it would only take a few minutes to the motel. What's more, the driver seemed to be getting more agitated by the second. His face screwed up so much he looked like he only had one eye. A bit like a taxi driving Cyclops with extremely bad body odour.

'Everything OK?' I asked.

'Where's hotel?' he replied.

I shrugged my shoulders. How the fuck did I know where the hotel was? I thought, 'You're supposed to be the fuckin' taxi driver.' I showed him the name on the piece of paper. I glanced at his badge on the dashboard. I couldn't pronounce his name, but I'm sure his photo had police numbers under it!

I couldn't tell if he was conning me even more, or if he was genuinely lost. But whatever it was, he was pissing me off now. I didn't mind forking out a few bucks extra to help feed his wife, thirteen kids, and probably his one-hundred-and-fifty-four-year-old grandmother, but I had a terrible feeling it was about to turn nasty.

'Give me phone... give me phone,' he sounded like he was mugging me. He reached behind to try to grab it.

'No!' I backed into the corner.

'Phone motel... you phone motel.'

'Oh, right.' I realised he was asking me to find out where it was. Maybe I had been wrong about him; maybe he was a nice guy. Yeah, and maybe my name was Rudolph Nureyev and I was off to my next ballet!

I called the motel.

'If you see a blue, rusty, bridge,' the receptionist told me, 'you have gone too far.'

Shit, we were actually on the bridge. The motel was about a quarter of a mile back. 'It's back there... you passed it.' I pointed over my shoulder. 'It's back there.'

He looked like I had just told him he had cancer of the nuts, or that I was giving him a bar of soap for Christmas. He shook his head. 'That will be one hundred dollars!' he screamed at me.

'What?' Another déjà vu moment. The only difference being his demands had got more expensive. 'Stop the cab!' I yelled at him. 'Stop the cab.'

He did what he was told. We both jumped out. He started shouting and swearing, sticking his face into mine. I threw him twenty bucks... 'That's all you're having mate... now fuck off!' I'm not a violent or a particularly brave person, but I stood there fuming. In my home town, taxi drivers got beaten up just for putting the meter on, or for not pulling up right outside someone's front door.

I glared at him, again trying to look kind of tough. 'Come on then, mate, if you think you are hard enough,' I said to myself.

Next thing, he leant into the glove compartment and pulled out a gun. 'Fucking hell,' I cried out and ran without looking back.

I sprinted over the bridge in the direction we had come from. The car horns blared as I zigzagged in and out of the oncoming traffic. Their headlights lit up my face. I darted up an alleyway, into a side street. When I thought I was safe, I stopped running. My heart pounded in my chest, my legs felt like jelly.

I punched the air. I had taken on the mad hitman taxi driver of Newark on his home patch, and beaten the money-grabbin' bastard. I couldn't wait to tell Tom the Terminator when I got back home.

Smirking to myself, I slowly walked towards the broken neon sign of the motel. It was only when I looked around that it dawned on me that I was in more trouble than ever. I was the wrong colour, in the wrong part of town, at the wrong time, and in the wrong whatever else I wanted to add to the wrong situation.

They appeared out of the shadows, staggering towards me. Like zombie creatures from the Michael Jackson's *Thriller* video. One deranged woman pushed a shopping trolley. I felt as if I was floating in the air, watching myself as the lead role in some kind of movie. In my mind I was sure I could hear the low murmur of the gutter people chanting. 'Fee-fi-fo-fum, I smell the fear of a businessman!'

I stood frozen to the spot. A gun shot rang out behind me. I screamed and put my hands over my head. OK, it was probably a car exhaust backfiring, but I didn't stick around to find out. I ran again, only this time much faster.

I sprinted around the corner; I could see the sign for the motel in the distance. In my imagination, I could feel their breath on my neck and their hands touching my skin.

I barged into the reception area, nearly knocking the door off its hinges. Everyone in there stopped to look at me.

Three prostitutes sitting on a worn-out sofa in the corner smiled at me. One uncrossed her legs. I swear it looked like a cave at Cheddar Gorge. To be honest, if I was smaller, I would have crawled up there and hidden in the safety of her nether regions. It may have looked dirty and smelt of cheese but it looked like the safest place to be at that moment.

I paid the receptionist and got my key. I couldn't get to my room quickly enough. I walked across the outside wooden corridor, eyes fixed to the floor. I passed a couple arguing. The big black guy slapped the woman across the face. She started to fight back.

'Never get involved in domestics,' was a motto I always stuck by. As he held her in a headlock, I slipped past. Inside my room, I locked the door. Now I felt more scared than ever, because now I had nowhere to run, nowhere to hide. I was stuck in the small, stinking room. My mind did cartwheels. I pictured the taxi driver kicking the door open, the zombie people on his shoulder. I dared not sleep. I curled up in a ball on the bed, cwtching into my computer, knees up to my chest.

I cursed everyone for putting me in this situation – BA, my business, the taxi driver, even my father for getting my mother pregnant after a dance in the Catholic hall in 1961. They were all to fuckin' blame.

Eventually I must have dropped off because I woke up with the grunting sound of someone, or something, having sex next door. The walls were so paper thin that I could hear every moan and groan, every bump and grind. It sounded like a monkey shagging a donkey, with a parrot commentating. I wondered if someone had been desperate enough to enter the prostitute with the dirty cave and the dirtier smile. When the monkey came, I felt like throwing up. Maybe my mystery lovers from Yarm had secretly followed me here and were giving me a special treat.

The guy on reception booked me another taxi. I couldn't believe it when it turned up. Fucking trust my luck, it was the same mental driver who had chased me with the gun. No, it wasn't, but the way my luck was going, I wouldn't have been surprised.

At the airport I called my contact in Cleveland to tell him what had happened. A shiver ran down my spine when he simply said I must be the luckiest man alive to have got out of that neighbourhood in one piece. 'They must have thought you were more nuts than them.' He didn't laugh.

But I had survived. I sat on the Virgin flight home. Safe and warm, nothing could upset me now. Then I turned to my side. The guy next to me smiled, his teeth whiter than white. 'Hello, friend.' He clutched an old worn-out Bible.

'Arrrgggggggggggggggggggghhhhhhhhhhhhhhhhhhhhh, fuckin' hell's bells.' My worst nightmare, another six-hour flight, with another religious maniac.

I'm a fuckin writer get me outta here!

16

Things Go Partner-shaped!

AFTER TEN YEARS or so of living in the fast-lane, mentally and physically, I began to fray around the edges. The type of lifestyle I lived took its toll. Weeks, sometimes months, passed without me seeing anyone else from the business. One year for example, I worked with Pete in the early January, and then didn't see him again until Christmas.

Nearly one hundred per cent of the time I worked alone. And although I'm quite happy to be a loner, even someone like me needed some human contact every now and then. The longer it went on, the more I got wrapped up in my own little shell. A social outcast housed up in a Travelodge from Sunday night until Friday; like a prisoner locked away in a cell in solitary confinement; lying there in my bunk scraping the days left into the plasterboard. Fortunately, I didn't have to shit in a bucket or be aware of large, horny, tattooed inmates in the showers.

On more than one occasion I talked to the furniture. Honest to God, me and Bernard, the two-door cupboard with three small drawers, sat there discussing everything from the football to did we find the kettle sexy?

When I did escape and go home, my family didn't understand or appreciate the way I was living, or surviving, while spreading the word of 'consultantism'. It was hard to adjust. (My pissing in the sink routine being a good example of that.)

I longed for normality back in my life – whatever normality meant. My work-life balance didn't balance at all. Every month,

I spent at least twenty days away from home. I worked out that in one year I slept in hotel rooms four times more than I slept in my own bed. I know the pillows were better, but that was ridiculous. I did that for several years on the tamp.

My young family never saw me. Looking back now, I do regret missing out on doing lots of normal family stuff with them. Being there on the actual day of my daughter's birthdays for one; or when they didn't feel well, or going to their teacher-parents meetings. Even silly things like Halloween and Bonfire Nights.

I am not going to deny the money was good. And to be truthful, as long as my family had a credit card, my dog Lucky was probably the only one in my house that missed me. (Only joking... well, I hope I am!)

It was a tough rut to climb out of.

But maybe, more worryingly, I developed other traits while on the road which had more serious and damaging side-effects.

I never thought I was on the verge of ever becoming a fully-blown alcoholic. Alcoholics never do, do they! But the way I was heading I wasn't far off. I worked on a long assignment up at Ellesmere Port, near Liverpool. Every night, without fail, I ventured from my hotel across a small, wooden lock over the canal to eat at a great South African restaurant.

It started off innocently enough with a glass or two of wine with dinner. I'd sit alone in the corner, writing stories while watching the world go by. Pretty soon, it progressed from two glasses to a bottle, then to a bottle and a half. One night, I topped the two-bottle limit. How I balanced back across the small wooden lock, I really can't remember. I think I ended up arguing with Bernard the cupboard about the benefits of countersunk screws or something equally daft!

My head the next morning belonged to someone else. And that someone else was a ninety-five-year-old tramp with cider for blood and a furry tongue.

I don't think my job suffered. (Well, that's what I told

myself.) My writing definitely didn't. Each night my mind came alive with creative ideas as the red vino flowed.

Frankly I wasn't in a good place. I craved for a drink most nights. It didn't stop there. As soon as I got home on a Friday, I'd crack open another couple of bottles. I've always prided myself on keeping fit. But I found myself making up every excuse under the sun why I couldn't go to the gym and why I needed to go for a drink instead. I also piled on the pounds. I felt sluggish and lethargic.

There had to be something more than me just staring at hotel walls, or at the bottom of an empty wine glass, or having arguments with my imaginary Formica chipboard friend. I knew something had to change. Either that or I'd end up a twenty-stone piss-head, or worse.

Sometimes, when driving home bored, I used to do some stupid things. My life turned into a big game of 'dare'. A few other consultants and I used to challenge each other while bombing along country lanes, normally somewhere in north Wales.

'The only way to show you are a true consultant is when you can do the following three things at the same time,' Joe used to brag.

The dare list was as follows:
Drive at 80 m.p.h. on a winding road in north Wales;
While on the phone – not hands-free;
And while eating a Burger King triple XXX cheeseburger with extra bacon and chili sauce – without getting any on your trousers.

Of course it was stupid. But still funny. Well, until the night I was driving home, alone (at normal speed, and not eating anything) and I witnessed a head-on crash. Nothing to do with me, I must add. As I slowly drove past, I saw a dying man being given the kiss of life right there on the side of the road. From that moment on, my messing about in the car days were well and truly over.

Probably my oddest foible had to do with pillows. It's

funny how boredom and soft pillows can turn an innocent person into a hardened (or softened) criminal. Like I revealed earlier, I don't know what it is about hotel pillows that make them so good. Why are they ten million times better than any pillow I've ever been able to buy? The ones at home turned into flat, hard pancakes after a week of sleeping on them. Even that woman in Ohio with the fifteen-stone head could sleep on a Premier Inn pillow for three months solid and it would still look and feel like new. She would probably have covered it in sugar and tried to eat it though, but that's another story.

I longed for that type of hotel pillow comfort in my life.

A terrible thing to admit now but, to get it, I decided to 'borrow' a pillow from a Premier Inn in Sheffield. I couldn't help myself. It was just so soft. It had been like sleeping on a cloud. Next morning, I wrapped it up in my coat and walked out. Problem was when I took it home, my family loved it too. One of them pinched it off me.

It got to the point where they talked me into 'borrowing' an additional seven pillows. Two for each of us.

I made a plan. Clockwork Pillow I called the operation. I took an empty kit bag whenever I stayed in the Premier Inn. Systematically, I acquired the pillows I needed. One morning I nearly got caught when the fluffiness of the pillow popped the zipper of the bag. Luckily no one saw it. I imagined my mugshot displayed in Premier Inns up and down the country. A wanted poster of me all over the walls like a mean cattle rustler in cowboy days.

Anthony Bunko – Wanted for Pillow Pinching, taking all the sugars and other hideous crimes!

After I smuggled out the seventh, I thought my pillow pirating days were over. But it didn't end there. It never does. My wife told her mother. She wanted some. She told her friend. They wanted some. Suddenly I had a list. I turned into the Howard 'fucking' Marks of the stolen pillow world.

It got out of control.

'Hey darling, the couple from number 46 would like two pillows and they wonder if you could get them a good mattress and a teasmaid.'

But seriously, in the end I used to follow the cleaning ladies down the corridor like Jack the Pillow Thief. To add to my roll of shame I also 'collected' wine glasses from the bars. Again, there is something about a good wine glass from hotels which are unlike anything you can buy.

I know it was wrong, but hey, Premier Inn is a massive organisation. They could afford the odd lost pillow or twenty-seven. They could tell their insurance company Lenny Henry ate the bloody things.

If caught, I would have told the judge my criminal activities started because of all the stress I was under from dealing with demanding idiots on a daily basis. And to me most of the stress came from inside our own company!

After being on the road for ages, I came back to find the business bent completely out of shape. I attended a two-day meeting and hardly recognised it any more. Gone was the smell of intellect and friendless I had witnessed when I first joined the business. A new breed of consultant had ridden into town wearing crocodile boots with alligator smiles. They brought with them a language more complicated and harder to understand than Welsh. Where we once prided ourselves on telling clients we didn't speak in jargon, now we were suddenly driving through Jargon City in a Sinclair C5 car. I didn't know what the fuck was going on.

'Take it to the BMT?' someone said in the meeting.

I'd never heard of the BMT. I was still trying to work out that it meant Business Management Team when someone else piped up, 'Never mind the BMT, shouldn't that be discussed at the MMM (Monthly Management Meeting) or the GMM (General Management Meeting)?'

'No, it is definitely a BMT issue.'

Acronyms flew around everywhere. I sat there completely confused. I considered taking a First World War code breaker course, just so I could understand what they were talking about.

'Surely it's a PMT matter,' said the woman who ran Human Resources.

I burst out laughing. Everyone looked at me. I felt like that first day I had joined. I didn't know anyone any more.

And that wasn't the worst of it. The atmosphere had become all grey and dull. To me it felt like a gang of storm troopers had invaded Oz and had hung the wizard up from the nearest lamp post by his ears. There seemed to be a lot of little cliques forming. Lots of in-fighting and politics crept in. No one seemed to have a good word to say about anyone. Even the girls in the office had split into smaller factions after a 'girly' argument went too far.

Discussions in meetings went on forever without any outcome. There was no fun, no pleasure at all, just excruciating pain. When I first started I used to look forward to business reviews. Now I hated them with a passion. I hated what they represented.

It felt like everyone wanted to be the big hero of the business, the centre-forward scoring all the goals and taking all the corners and free-kicks. Individuals openly lopped their members out on the desk (even the office girls) to brag how big their tools were. 'My todger is the biggest. Now give me more money.' They all bragged themselves up like fishermen boasting about the size of their catch. It was all a bit like the four Yorkshiremen sketch by Monty Python.

I've sold sixty-thousand pounds worth of business today... I'm the best.

Only sixty... I sold ninety grand, plus a holiday for two in Lanzarote.

I wouldn't get out of bed for ninety grand and a holiday for two in Lanzarote. I just sold a five million pound intervention, starting in two weeks, involving eleven hundred consultants, and their wives, children, and pets... and a holiday for six in Jamaica.

I wouldn't put my slippers on for a five million pound intervention...

And on, and on, and on it went.

I hated it. Greed became an evil bedfellow. I'd heard individuals openly talk about fiddling their taxes. After a few years of doing my books I got rather blasé about it, but I never fiddled. OK, if I'm truthful I did pick up someone else's receipt from the floor in Burger King once in a while. But that was all. I'd heard a rumour that one guy in the business claimed his pet rabbit, Fluffy Jones, was his secretary. Another one declared to the taxman his mother-in-law put all his presentations together and booked his hotel rooms and stuff. Thing was, she had been dead for four years!

For a brief moment I did consider asking the consultant with the rabbit if Fluffy could do my books as well. But by then he had been eaten by the next door's dog, which probably worked for the taxman!

I didn't know what had happened to the people I had met on my first day of walking into the business. Where had the supply teachers with the patches on their jackets gone? What about The Trainspotter? I didn't recognise anyone any more. Even The 1970s Porn Star had shaved off his 1970s porno moustache and didn't wear tight trousers anymore, for fuck's sake!

However, the main partners still stood out the front, saying basically the same stuff they had preached on my first day there. But now it had lost its mojo.

'We must grow or die, a painful and horrible death,' The 5-Star Gimp did his *Springtime for Hitler* routine. He still looked alarmingly war-like, his moustache bigger and more intimidating than ever as he marched about.

'We are all great, especially me!' chipped in The Glass Is Always Half Full partner with a double smile on his normally happy face.

'I am The Prof, I am The Egg-man,' announced The Prof. He even had a T-shirt with his face on it. He seemed to have gone off his rocker by this point, and I didn't know what the fuck he was going on about.

The Master had retired. He'd had enough. I didn't think he would ever go, unless carried out in a pine box with the words 'Don't let fuckin' Chris anywhere near me, or I will come back and haunt the fuckin' lot of you' printed on the side. Although he had been a pedantic bastard most of the time, he did steady the ship. Sometimes, he steered it towards the rocks and the sharks, but he was never afraid to admit when he got it wrong, and would turn it around.

If it weren't for him, I wouldn't have been half the consultant I became. He saw something inside me; some deep-rooted potential waiting to burst out. He once sat me down and said, 'Anthony, I'm quite good at reading people, but I haven't got a fucking clue what goes on in your mind. You're a complete mystery to me.'

A massive compliment... I think!!

With him not about, mayhem and lawlessness took over. 'Anarchy in the BS,' Johnny Rotten would have sung if he had been a consultant.

Everywhere I looked the proud golden rules of the business had subconsciously altered to the following:

*1. No consultants shall wear fancy clothes and watches **to bed**.*

*2. No consultant shall drive posh flash cars **too fast**.*

*3. No consultant shall drink alcohol on a school night **to excess**.*

*4. No consultants shall bad-mouth any consultant **unless they have good cause**.*

5. All consultants are equal, but some consultants are more equal than others and the partners are better than that again.

The days of driving 'normal' cars had disappeared too. The partners led by example and bombed around the country in top of the range BMWs, flashy sports cars, and expensive Jeeps.

Every meeting I went to we just seemed to do the

same things. It was all a bit like *Groundhog Day*, a bit like *Groundhog Day*. We talked about the same nonsense. Talk and more talk with little doing. We even told the same boring jokes. We were forever writing lists of bullshit on flip charts and covering the walls with Post-it notes. I was, and still am, convinced all consultants have shares in flip chart and Post-it making companies. We created lists and lists of stuff we never got around to doing.

One time, after a full day of flip charting, I was given the task of taking the 'very, very important outcomes' back to the office to get them typed up. I'm not sure what happened, but I lost them all. Maybe, subconsciously, I threw them in the River Taff, or burnt them in a wheelie bin. I'm not saying! But the best thing was, no one ever noticed. No one ever asked me about them. A few months later we did the same exercise again. And better still, this time we came up with a different set of outcomes.

To stop me from beating someone to death with a lump hammer at these meetings, I used to sit at the back and play Bollocks Bingo with some of the other 'sane' consultants (there weren't many left). The rules were simple. Each of us would write ten consultant words or phrases down on a piece of paper. Things like *paradigm-shift* (which to be honest I thought was the name of a cough sweet). Other, well-used consultant bollocks words – like *framework, heads-up, outside the box, linkage, low hanging fruit, mobilization, helicopter view, transformation, dashboard, culture change, agile* – were spouted out, along with a million others.

Exactly like bingo, when someone mentioned the words during the presentations, the aim was to cross them off the list faster than anyone else. The record was six minutes. Six fucking minutes before Tom crossed off the ten words on his list. Six fucking minutes, that's how much bullshit was being bandied about. The culprit that day was, of course, The Glass Is Always Half Full partner, talking about changing the culture of a business (not our business, of course, that didn't need changing!) while riding a tricycle and juggling five flip chart markers at the same time.

Tom was happy. He won a cuddly bear and a box of chocolates.

I got to the point where I dreaded going to any internal meetings at all. I'd have nightmares the night before. I'd wake up in a cold sweat after imagining being chased around a hotel lobby by consultants with huge heads, waving handfuls of cash at me and talking like nineteenth-century druids.

The sad thing was we never talked to each other any more, well not in English anyway. Every break and lunchtime, everyone jumped on their computers and hurriedly sent emails which they should have done yesterday. We stopped communicating with each other. Just like teenagers addicted to their mobiles, we were the same on our computers. We would send an email to someone who was sitting in the same fucking room, in the next fucking chair.

After a while, I purposely didn't take my computer with me to the meetings. I wanted to sit and talk. I didn't see any of them from one month to the other. While they were busy sending the last great email, I used to go for a walk around the gardens, or sit in my car listening to the radio.

At the end of the day we always finished with a round-the-room discussion on what individuals thought of the day.

The Glass Is Always Half Full partner always started it off with his stock answers. 'Brilliant... best ever. I think we have made a giant leap as a business today. And we have really laid down the foundations for other business meetings.'

The Prof normally rubbed his chin in a very thoughtful way and profoundly added, 'In all my years of being a Prof... that was the best meeting I've ever been in. Blah, blah, blah,' with an extra-long 'blahhhhhhhh' to finish.

The 5-Star Gimp would goose-step across the table while swinging two imaginary twelve-inch black, rubber dildos above his head.

Everyone would nod their heads in agreement and chip in with some sycophantic comment.

If I had the balls, I would have said what I really felt. 'We talked bullshit all day.' Alas, I didn't. My stock answer was always, 'Yeah, it was OK.'

But, in truth, it sapped my creative energy, and left me with a bad head.

I know I wasn't the innocent party in all this. I wanted different things by then. It got to the point where I hated the sight of most of them. It was like a relationship gone sour. Their voices ground at my insides. Their smug attitudes got under my skin.

Most of the partners wanted us to conquer the world. (Of course, The 5-Star Gimp was the ring leader.) We had a partners' meeting to discuss our strategy for the next five years. It was beyond cruel. The height of cruelty!

'We will not only double our sales but we will quadruple our profits,' The 5-Star General's moustache twitched excitedly as he told us the top secret plan, which everyone knew about anyway.

I couldn't fault their ambition. What I did question were the motives for driving the business so hard. To me it was down to one thing – greed. The other questionable flaw in their scheme was our lack of ability to actually achieve what they wanted.

A few years before, we had announced to the troops at BS Consulting an all-singing, all-dancing workshop of how we were going to grow to a ten million pound operation by 2010 (a neat 'ten by ten' slogan was used constantly).

'This will make us rich,' The Prof told the already bored group of consultants. What he should have said was, 'This will make the partners rich, and will mean you will have to work your balls off to hit our targets.'

Three years later, the business had gone backwards. We were nowhere near the ten million pound target. In fact, we were worse than we were when we had announced the growth. But now, we had a spiralling wage bill, a frustrated workforce who all wanted a share of the pie but couldn't get any, and lower profits. The partners blamed the consultants. The consultants blamed the partners. I think some people actually laid some of the blame on the girls in the office. That was how bad it got. Not a nice place to work.

In my opinion if we, the partners, had been eleven 'Moseses', there wouldn't have been any Promised Land. We may have talked a good fight and thought a good game, but the Jews would have probably all ended up living in a two-up, two-down council house on the outskirts of Leeds.

Yet, two years on, and here we were insisting we should be out to conquer the world, yet again. The way we were heading, we couldn't conquer a sweet shop in fuckin' Bristol.

'Let's go for twenty million pounds by 2015,' said The Glass Is Always Half Full partner.

Had they gone mad? Had I gone deaf maybe and heard them wrong? I laughed out loud.

They looked at me.

'Guys, you couldn't get to ten million... how the hell are you going to get to twenty?'

Arrows in the hat time for me. I got beaten from every corner. I shut up and let them continue. By then I had made a conscious decision to step away from all the internal politics and dick-measuring. My plan was to latch onto a big client contract, and bury my head in their sand until everything blew over, or the end of the world came!

17

The Turd of King Kong

WRITING MAD THINGS proved to be my mechanism for getting out of the madness. Maybe it was also my own unique way of getting through a mid-life crisis. While some of my forty-year-old mates were getting tattoos of dragons, or buying motorbikes, I picked up a pen, and wrapped up warm with my imagination.

It kept me sane (or insane) during that period. In truth, I got quite prolific at it. Book after book I churned out. Looking back now, I believe there had always been a little spark inside me. I just needed something creative to set it alight.

And within no time it did.

I ran a workshop in the steel mill from hell. Dressed up like a spaceman, I wandered about aimlessly trying not to get killed. It was without doubt like being in the fires of hell. Heat, flames and evil little demons lurked in every corner. Signs hung everywhere which basically stated, 'Don't do that or you will die... death around next corner... you are going to die, die and die.'

I was scared shitless. The noise and the heat were unbearable. I couldn't hear a word I was saying. The sweat crept down the cheeks of my arse like a sneaky robber tiptoeing his way across the floor of an art gallery.

'Let's have a water break,' I gestured to the others.

'What time should we come back?' one guy asked.

I wanted to say, 'Never.'

I put my five fingers up four times.

I went for a walk to cool down and get my hearing back. In the fresh-ish air I noticed eight missed calls from home. In a panic, I called back. My wife excitedly told me a film director from LA had called. He wanted me to call him back. Apparently, through a friend of a friend, he had read my book about a spider and a fly falling in love in Dublin docks, and loved it!

His name was Gary Chapman. I quickly Googled him and found out he had directed the British animated movie *Valiant*, starring Ewan McGregor, and many other top British actors. With hands shaking, as much from the cold as anything else, I phoned him back. I didn't even consider how much it would cost to call LA on my mobile.

He wanted me to fly out to see him as soon as possible. I couldn't believe it. Me, going from Cardiff docks to LA, within the blink of an eye. I immediately cancelled some appointments, and flew out within two days. I didn't care what the partners thought.

I didn't have a clue what he looked like, other than seeing him on YouTube at the premier of the *Valiant* movie. He picked me up from the airport in his Jeep. He looked very rock and roll. The sun was shining as I drove past the giant Hollywood sign located on the hill. I had to pinch myself to make sure I wasn't dreaming.

I spent a week living with him, travelling around, meeting people, getting drunk, and talking about the book. He had a great imagination. We fed off each other. We turned the book into a film script. Sadly, nothing came of it but, more importantly, it gave me a taste of a different world. A world I wanted to sample every day of my life.

Not long after, I had another stroke of luck.

By accident, I met Stuart Cable, ex-drummer with one of the biggest groups in the UK, the Stereophonics. I ended up in Stuart's mansion. I walked around his house in awe staring at all his gold discs hanging on the wall, and the Brit Award the band had won, years earlier, for Best Newcomer.

Writing was my passion, but music will always be my first love.

Stuart enchanted me with stories about the band. One of

the tales was the now infamous story about how he ate Keith Richards' shepherd's pie while the boys supported the Stones in Paris. Apparently Mick Jagger found out, and full of devilry, rushed off to inform Keith.

Being rather drunk by then, I asked Stuart if I could write his life story. Unbelievably, he agreed. We shook hands on it there and then. The next morning, when I woke up, I thought, 'Fucking hell... I hope he's forgotten about it.' Two hours later, he called me up. His booming Welsh voice overpowering my phone. 'I've spoken to my manager Butt (John Brand the ex-manager of the Stereophonics) and he said let's go for it. But he wants to see some chapters first.'

That's when panic hit me. How the hell was I going to write a rock star's life story? Writing fiction books I found easy. There weren't any real rules to them. OK, there are rules, but not like putting together an autobiography. I rushed down the library to get some books on other famous people. I spent two days reading about eight of them.

Again, the punk attitude inside me took over. I thought, 'Let's give it a go. What have I got to lose?'

I met up with Stuart two days later in his local. I wrote the outline of his life and a sample chapter in two days. Within a week we got a deal with a major London-based publishing house. Understandably, I was over the moon. That night I had more than a few red wines, let me tell you.

Although I was still working, and flying all over the world, every spare minute of my day I set about writing the book. I used some of my holidays to meet with Stuart. Normally we sat in his local. The both of us would drink, and drink. He would talk, and talk, while I took notes. Every session, more often than not, ended up with us going back to his house and drinking more. I would always wake up in his spare room with an almighty hangover.

Then came the hard work of me sobering up and writing the bloody thing.

He took me everywhere with him; the Kerrang Awards,

where we stayed in some posh hotel in London along with Metallica and Rage Against the Machine (although I wasn't a big fan of either).

Later, I hooked up with Welsh rugby superstars like Scott Gibbs and Jonathan Davies, plus I became good mates with the Dirty Sanchez boys. I also met the infamous drug lord, who turned out to be one of the nicest guys in the world, Howard Marks. We are still mates.

One of the best nights saw me partying backstage, and later in a Cardiff hotel until the early hours, with Liam and Noel Gallagher from Oasis. It was surreal. My wife called me at 5.30 in the morning and asked where the hell I was. (Let's just say her words were a little more colourful.)

'I'm sitting in St David's Hotel talking about the Sex Pistols with Liam Gallagher.'

'Fuck off,' she replied.

Liam took the phone off me and talked to her. When he handed it back she said, 'OK, I'll see you when you get home. Bye.' For once, she was lost for words.

Whatever people say, and whatever you read about the brothers, I found them to be top blokes. Very welcoming, engaging and extremely funny people.

By the March we had a big book launch in a nightclub, in the heart of Cardiff. I was so proud of it. It had been serialised in the *Western Mail*. Stu had been interviewed on TV shows about it. The shepherd's pie story even made it onto *Loose Women*.

I took a copy to the next partnership meeting. The partners avoided it like the plague. They didn't even look at it. I think they did it for two reasons. One, they could tell how passionate I was about it. I think they thought I had done it in work's time, which wasn't true! I had written the book while still giving one hundred per cent to the business. I found the time. Even if it meant staying awake in my hotel until 3 a.m. in the morning.

The second reason, deep-down, I think was that some of them were a little jealous. I think they all thought they were more intelligent than me.

By then I didn't care less what they thought. The book opened lots of doors for me. It was only then that I knew the writing was really and truly on the wall.

I was very happy outside work, and very unhappy in work. Slowly, I went into my shell. I started to hate getting up in the mornings, and I couldn't wait until Friday arrived. It was like turning the clock back to my days at the steering column company.

Of course, part of the problem was me falling out of love with it all. I knew that. I had revved off track completely. While the partners were bombing along on the M1 in flashy BMWs looking to conquer all before them, little old me was content to go ambling along in a VW camper van in the middle of a dusty, old, riverside road.

The beginning of the end started not long after Stuart's book release.

*

Poland was one of the straws that broke the consultant's flip chart. I had been asked at very short notice to travel to a large electronics factory churning out TV sets about two hours outside Warsaw. One of our consultants had screwed up while running a workshop and I was asked to go and rescue the situation.

One of the secretaries in the office sorted out flights and accommodation and emailed me all the details. I quickly packed a bag and caught a plane out of Heathrow.

I'd never been to Poland before. The only things I really knew about the country were Warsaw, union shipbuilders with giant moustaches, and a footballer called Lato scoring a goal against England to knock them out of the World Cup.

On flying into Lech Walesa airport, a little, devious part of me wanted all the aeroplanes on the runway to have giant, black moustaches under the cockpit. Predictably, and rather disappointingly, they didn't.

An upbeat, cheerful, Polish taxi driver (without a moustache, by the way) picked me up. With great pride he told me all about the business he had built up and how he loved people from the United Kingdom – they were the best. I bet he said that to all his clients, well maybe not the Germans!

During the journey he asked me what hotel I was staying in. I handed him the slip of paper with the name written on it. I don't read body language but if I did his would have screamed out, 'You must be f'ing joking, my little Welsh leek.'

'Is it OK?' I nervously laughed.

'Are you really staying there?' he asked.

I nodded. The girl from our office told me there had been some business conference in the small town and the hotel was all she could get. The driver shrugged and drove on.

Oh no, all this shrugging could only mean one thing.

At around 10 p.m. we finally reached the old town. Everything seemed peaceful. All the cafés and bars looked empty. Perhaps the fact that most of the people from Poland were now walking around my hometown on a Friday afternoon could explain why there wasn't anyone about.

The driver looked kind of embarrassed when he stopped the car in front of the poorly-lit hotel.

'Welcome to Hell,' it should have said above the door.

'Fuck me.' I stood with my case outside the main entrance to what was basically a doss house. And a very, low market, doss house at that. However, it had been a long trip and I only needed a bed and a piece of toast in the morning. How bad could it be?

I found out as soon as I entered the foyer. The carpet was threadbare and filthy. Paint peeled off the walls. The place smelt of sweaty armpits. I rang the small bell on the reception desk. A girl appeared – overweight and dressed in grubby-looking clothes. Worst of all, a series of boils on her arms and face wouldn't have looked out of place on an old hag during the Black Plague. On my life, they looked so bad, I recoiled in disgust. A few of them wept with yellow puss. The one on her forehead looked as if it had come to life.

'Excuse me,' I gulped, 'I'm booked in here for a few nights.'

A set of rotten teeth tried to smile back at me. She looked so ugly she should have come with a warning and a double-bag. 'Do you want me to make you a sandwich?' she asked in broken English.

Even though I was starving I would have rather eaten my own ear wax (or someone else's ear wax, well except hers). 'Forget feeding me, go to the nearest VD clinic and get yourself checked out, quickly,' I wanted to tell her.

I declined her kind offer of grub.

Another older woman turned up in similar filthy-looking clothes. There must have been a sale on at the Filthy Clothes boutique. To be fair to her, she had less boils on her face but her teeth were greener. 'That will be seven billion zonts,' she said, or whatever the currency was, and glared at me. Her eyebrows touched in the middle like a young Noel Gallagher before he had his one giant brow surgically parted in the middle.

'You pay now,' her hand outstretched.

She reminded me of the waitress from the Chinese restaurant in my hometown, Hing Hongs, the most bizarre Chinese restaurant in the history of Chinese restaurants. Knives weren't allowed, unless carried by the waitresses themselves. Every meal came with a fried egg on top and if anyone asked for Chinese tea they got banned. To top it all, customers were made to pay before they were given their meal. Thus the comparison.

I handed the less boil-ridden woman my credit card. I didn't argue, I just wanted to get to bed. My room was located right on the top floor of the rickety, old building. Of course, there wasn't a lift. I was lucky there were stairs. An old guy passed me on the way up. He smelt like he'd pissed himself. A TV set blared out from somewhere. A man and woman screamed at each other from the room next to me.

I opened the door to my room. The bed was unmade. I checked the number on the door with the key. Number 16. It was the right room. The sound of the arguing next door grew louder. I closed the door and locked it. Without exaggerating it was the worst room I'd ever been in, in my entire life. The carpet was minging beyond belief. Both doors hung off the tiny cupboard in the corner. A hole in the plasterboard wall looked like someone had put their fist, or someone else's head, or both, through it.

I pulled back the bed sheets. I half-expected to see fleas or bugs or even an octopus crawling about. What I didn't expect to find was a grubby, white, stained vest rolled up in a ball among the sheets. Who did it belong to? How long had it been there for? Was he coming back for it?

If that wasn't bad enough, it got considerably worse when I opened the door to the bathroom. First off there was no bath, just a stinking sink and a toilet.

A log floating in the toilet bowl looked like King Kong had dumped it there after being on the Atkins diet for a month. I heaved. I flushed. It stayed there, refusing to be beaten. It taunted me with its big brown face. I heaved again. This time I spewed. My aeroplane meal spun around and around in the dirty sink. The turd of King Kong floating in the toilet bowl laughed at me.

I again wanted to cry. I'd had enough of it. Dirty vests and King Kong's poo was bad enough for any man to take.

I sat on the bed, head in my hands. Just then my phone rang. It was the woman running the session in the factory. She called to see if everything was all right.

'Where are you staying?' she asked.

'Hotel from Hell,' I replied. 'Hotel Ibac.'

She laughed. 'No seriously where are you staying?'

'I am deadly serious. Everything else was booked.'

'Oh... what is it like?'

I didn't know her well enough to tell her I had found a dead man's vest in my bed and King Kong had sneaked into my room and taken a dump. 'It's not good,' I replied. 'Even the cockroaches are checking out.'

'Give me five.' She hung up.

I waited. The arguing from the other room seemed to have turned into a full-blown scrap. Within a week I had gone from partying with the biggest rock band on the planet to sitting on the dirtiest hotel bed in history.

My contact rang back. 'Get your stuff and meet me downstairs in ten minutes.'

'Yessss,' I punched the air. I thought about taking the vest with me for a souvenir to show the guys when I got home, but it was just too disgusting.

I raced down to the reception. 'I'm not staying here,' I told the two boil-laden witches. 'I want my money back.'

The older one shook her head. She pretended not to understand me.

'Oh fuck you,' I glared at her, 'I hope your boils have boils.'

I met the woman in her car outside. She took me to a great, family-owned hotel. But the experience had again scarred me. The pressure and demands of being a high-flying, bullshit-talking consultant was taking its toll. A week or so later, one of my colleagues resigned after a nightmare assignment to Mexico. In tears, he told me how he had crossed over the border from El Paso to Juarez in a car with blacked-out windows. Juarez was not only the murder and cocaine smuggling capital of the world, but also the 'missing limbs for cash' and human-trafficking capital as well. He went out for a meal and had to have bodyguards standing by the door holding AK37 machine guns.

'I'm a consultant, not a fucking drug lord!' he said. He left the business soon after.

All eyes turned to me to pick up the work. 'Fuck off,' I told them. I was sick of being the 'fly me in to cover up others' mistakes' consultant. And I wasn't going to get kidnapped and lose a kidney, or an eye, or worse still, my penis, in the name of Lean! The only way I was going to go to Mexico was if I was lying on a beach in Cancun, holding a margarita and reading a book.

The final, final straw that smashed the flip chart to bits came in the shape of a partners' team-building day. By then I thought it was broken beyond all repair. I personally felt so removed from the others I may as well have been living in outer space, or Outer Mongolia.

The atmosphere between everybody had got quite malicious – like rival football fans standing on a railway station waiting for something to kick off. The bad mood filtered like a disease into the rest of the business.

So another, 'softer' consultancy group had been hired by HR to get the partner team to start performing like a team. The partners' team-building day took place in the forest near Ross-on-Wye. It didn't even start well. The 5-Star Gimp rode up on an imaginary Arab charger thinking we were going to war. He started directing operations to the annoyance of the other trainers before we had done anything. The Glass Is Always Half Full partner was full of even more beans than ever. He bounced about like a kid, laughing and joking and clapping his hands. If I had a gun I would have shot him. The Prof looked scared. As though he was going to be asked to do something physical like climb a tree or balance across a log over a river. He informed everyone he had pulled something and sat out most of the activities on a large tree stump thinking. The brainy bastard!

The day soon deteriorated into the same farce we faced in our working lives. During a problem-solving exercise, a few 'senior' partners (The 5-Star Gimp as per usual) took over and told some of us 'not so senior' partners what to do, even though he didn't have a clue what was going on. Piss-up and brewery came to mind.

It suddenly broke into chaos. Screaming and yelling. It turned into violent personal tennis matches between individuals.

'Stop bossing us about,' one of newer consultant partners yelled at the Gimp-master, 'and help us!'

Fifteen-love.

'I'm not bossing you about,' The 5-Star Gimp said, his moustache twitched. 'Now hurry up and carry that log over there and...'

Fifteen-all.

'I'm warning you.'

Thirty-fifteen.

'Stop making a fool of yourself and just do as I say.'

Thirty-all.

'AARrrrrrgggggghhhhhhh,' the newer consultant partner sprinted at The 5-Star Gimp. 'I'm going to kill you...'

The Glass Is Always Full partner grabbed him around the leg to slow him down.

More shouting, more screaming. A truce was finally called. But the damage had already been done. In the end, everyone couldn't wait to get out of there and go home. I left the forest feeling more frustrated than before I went in. I wished a bear had leapt out of the bushes and eaten some of them, well, all of them. Sadly that didn't happen.

Nothing had been solved. It had gone a long way to making it worse. To me what the business was screaming out for was someone to take charge. Ideally, someone like Sir Alex Ferguson. Someone who couldn't care two fucks about reputations and how good a 'Thinker' someone was. Despondently, that was never going to happen.

I trooped through my front door looking like an American soldier trudging through a swamp in Vietnam.

That Friday night I typed out my resignation on my computer. My wife could tell something was wrong. I didn't go into detail, but I told her I wasn't happy and wanted out. To be fair, she's never stopped me if I wanted to move on. She's always believed in me. But even she was a little hesitant, due to the money I was making.

After a bottle, or two, of wine she said, 'It's up to you... I will back you.' Just then the phone in the other room rang. It was her mother. While she was on the phone, I went upstairs and sent my resignation by email to the partners along with a photo of a bird escaping out of a cage.

I came down the stairs with a big grin on my face. The weight of the world lifted off my shoulders. I always remember that next five minutes, as if it was five minutes ago.

'Why are you looking so happy?' my wife asked while sitting back on the settee clenching her glass of wine.

'I've done it.'

'Done what?'

'I've told them I'm finishing.'

She laughed, 'You haven't.'

'I have.'

There was a long pause, followed by a huge scream. My two daughters came running in. She told them what I had done. More huge screams escaped from all of them. It was hilarious. They all raced around the conservatory. 'We are going to be poor... we are going to be poor. It's your fault.' They started beating me up.

In my mind's eye, my wife and kids appeared like paupers begging on street corners for pennies.

But it was too late to go back. The deed had been done. As a matter of fact, I never went back to another partner or business review meeting. After that, I never spoke to half of the partners ever again.

I was on a year's notice. So I decided I would use it wisely. For my final year, I did what was needed to be done. I used the time to make some contacts and enjoy myself.

Within a week of handing in my notice (or emailing my notice in, to be more precise) my life changed. I got a call from a London publisher who asked would I be interested in writing a biography of Hugh Jackman, followed by a similar book about Hugh Laurie, plus others. And then, a little later, I was introduced to a wonderful woman, Anna Rodriguez, and I ended up writing her incredible life story, *Ma'am Anna*, about her fight against human trafficking. It was released to glowing reviews in the country that always eats... USA, of all places! And that was only the start.

Looking back now over ten years or so of being a consultant, I wouldn't change anything, mainly because I can't. It's over. So, as I close the page on that interesting chapter of my life, it made me think. Is there a moral to this story? Some kind of deep, underlying message, to take from all of this?

And there is.

The moral of this story is: Tell your careers officer to fuck off and mind his own business.

The Beginning

My two true facts and my one little white lie question:
I used to play drums in a punk rock band.
I have a three-legged dog called Lucky.
I won a Welsh international rugby cap.

The answer: Number one – I actually played bass guitar in a punk band (Crossed Wires), not the drums.

Thanks for reading. I hope you have enjoyed my little journey. Now I will leave you with a quote from a great man who inspired me, the scarecrow from *The Wizard of Oz:*

> *Some people without brains*
> *do an awful lot of talking, don't they?*

Thanks

I would like to thank the following people from the bottom of my heart:

- Jasper (Darren Woodland) for not only sponsoring me to write this book, but for also inviting me to many great parties and introducing me to the famous Big AL. I wish Jasper and his brilliant business, ECS, every success in the world.
- Mark Phillips for the brilliant cover design. Such a talented guy even though I'm a right pain in the arse.
- Lefi Gruffudd and all who sail in the good ship Y Lolfa for publishing the book.
- Eifion Jenkins for all the editing and poking me with a pointy stick in places where I needed to be poked!

Stay free
Bunko
X

Other titles by Anthony Bunko

Available at Amazon and all good and not-so-good bookshops

The Tale of the Shagging Monkeys

The Tale of Two Shagging Monkeys – The Siege of El Rancho

The Belt of Kings

TV, Tarot Cards and George 'bloody' Clooney

Working up to the Slaughterhouse (Poetry book)

Demons and Cocktails: My Life with the Stereophonics
(with Stuart Cable)

Hugh Laurie The Biography

Deadwalker

*Ma'am Anna: The Remarkable Story
of a Human Trafficking Rescuer*

Hugh Jackman The Biography

Spikey – 2 Hard to Handle The Autobiography of Mike Watkins
(with Mike Watkins)

www.anthonybunko.com

Lord Forgive Me… is just one of a whole range of publications from Y Lolfa. For a full list of books currently in print, send now for your free copy of our new full-colour catalogue. Or simply surf into our website

www.ylolfa.com

for secure on-line ordering.

TALYBONT CEREDIGION CYMRU SY24 5HE
e-mail ylolfa@ylolfa.com
website www.ylolfa.com
phone (01970) 832 304
fax 832 782